The New York Times
SURVEY SERIES

THEODORE M. BERNSTEIN
GENERAL EDITOR

THE NEW YORK TIMES Survey Series comprises books that deal comprehensively yet comprehensibly with subjects of wide interest, presenting the facts impartially and drawing conclusions honestly.

The series draws on the great information resources of *The New York Times* and on the talents, backgrounds and insights of specially qualified authors, mostly members of the *Times* staff.

The subjects range from the relatively particular problems of civilized life to the broadest conceivable problems concerning whether civilized life, or any kind of life, will continue to be possible on this planet.

The hope is that the books will be essentially informative, perhaps argumentative, but beyond that stimulative to useful, constructive thinking by the citizens who ultimately must share in civilization's decisions.

The
Black
Dilemma

JOHN HERBERS

The John Day Company
An Intext Publisher
NEW YORK

Published in hardcover by
The John Day Company, 257 Park Avenue South, New York, N.Y. 10010

Published in softcover by
Intext Press, 257 Park Avenue South, New York, N.Y. 10010

Published on the same day in Canada by Longman Canada Limited.

Printed in the United States of America

Library of Congress Cataloging in Publication Data

Herbers, John.
  The Black dilemma.

  (New York times survey series)
    1. Negroes–Civil rights. 2. Black power–United States. I. Title.
E185.615.H377   322.4'3'0973   72–2406
  ISBN: 0-381-98118-5 (hardcover)
          0-381-90001-0 (paperback)

Contents

Preface

EVER SINCE black people were brought to the shores of America there has been, both within their own community and within the larger society, a debate about who they were, how they were to fit into the American culture, and what would be their ultimate destiny. Other minorities, of course, have asked these same questions and heard them asked about themselves. But there can be no disagreement about the fact that the Negro American occupies a unique position in the society. He is the only one who came involuntarily and who, long after he arrived, was an instrument in making the American dream come true, not for himself, but for those who came voluntarily to seek it for themselves.

During the past two decades black Americans have made an extraordinary effort to put themselves on the same footing with other Americans, to place themselves in a position where they could choose their own destiny rather than have it chosen for them. It is natural, then, that the debate over what constitutes the proper place for blacks within the American society should have intensified and new ambiguities and misunderstandings arisen.

This book attempts to trace the history of Negro goals from the beginning of the nation through the tumultuous Negro revolution of the 1950's and 1960's. It makes no attempt to be a complete history or to touch upon every significant development. It does attempt to explain to some extent what seems to be the most important developments and to analyze their meaning. It relies mostly on what blacks say about themselves and their goals, as drawn from historical texts and hundreds of interviews, rather than the historic white interpretation of what it is all about. The discussion centers on the following list of goals, briefly defined:

Back to Africa—a colonization movement whereby American Negroes would migrate in groups and establish a new life in Africa, the continent of their origin many generations ago.

Nationalism—the belief that a race of people has a culture, language, ethnic identity, and way of life that are distinct from those of other groups and thus the race should set itself apart to preserve its identity, promulgate its own rules, and shape its own destiny.

Separatism—withdrawal from the larger society by a racial minority into its own cities, towns, communities, or neighborhoods, as far as it is practicable to do so.

Pluralism—the theory that American society is, and should be, made up of various ethnic, racial, and religious groups, each staying together but participating in the larger society.

Community Control—the idea of a racial minority segregated by choice or by circumstance within a community maintaining its own government, economy, and institutions, so far as it is possible to do so.

Integration—the act of members of a racial minority entering into the life and institutions of the larger society without regard to the race of the other participants.

Liberation—the idea that blacks not be totally committed

to any of the above but should employ each, or not, in a way that would best advance the race.

Hopefully, these ideas and movements are defined and placed in perspective for a better understanding of what blacks want.

JOHN HERBERS

February, 1972

The Black Dilemma

1

Back to Africa
with all the dumb Niggers

IN THE SPRING of 1970, a dozen Negro teen-agers from across the South were brought to Washington by civil rights groups to talk to members of Congress and officials in the Nixon Administration about massive integration that was scheduled to take place in the public schools in the fall. It had been sixteen years since the Supreme Court ruled that segregated education maintained by law and public policy was unconstitutional, and in that sixteen years—the full life-time of most of the dozen youths—there had been a national movement of major proportions in which America's black minority had struggled to break out of the discrimination and poverty that had bound Negroes for three hundred years.

Education was only one aspect of the struggle, but it was a major one, both substantively and symbolically. During the 1960's, civil rights leaders were heard to say frequently that the Emancipation Proclamation freed the bodies of black people and the 1954 Supreme Court decision, coming almost one hundred years later, freed their minds. Now, after a decade and a half of delay, violent opposition, and only partial implementation of the decision through judicial and

3

executive action, desegregation plans were maturing so that in thousands of schools in the South it appeared that there would be complete integration of white and Negro students. (Even though the Supreme Court had not decided whether neighborhood racial patterns in the major and medium-sized cities should limit the extent of integration, as the Nixon Administration advocated.)

This was the opportunity that a host of civil rights advocates had awaited, a milestone in the arduous effort to open American institutions and processes to Negroes, and particularly the black poor. Yet the teen-agers who came to Washington had been in integrated schools and they were somewhat embittered by the experience. The pattern, they said, was to continue the "white rules" and "white control" even in schools predominantly Negro. They complained of the playing of "Dixie" at football games, the exclusion of blacks from various school activities, the imposition of "dress and groom codes" that excluded Afro haircuts and dress, and the dismissal of black teachers who were said to be less qualified than whites.

The teen-agers were asking that the federal presence be increased so that black needs and demands would not be shunted aside in the process of massive integration. But beyond that they spoke with deep reservations about the chances of integration ever working at any level. The goal of the Negro movement, having been pursued at great cost and with good faith for so long, suddenly seemed hollow now that it was about to be achieved in a number of communities. A sixteen-year-old high school junior from South Carolina said, "Most kids feel integration is dead."

"How do you feel about it?" a reporter asked.

"It's dead," he replied without hesitation.

Mrs. Ruby Martin, former director of the Office of Civil Rights in the Department of Health, Education and Welfare, a Negro civil rights attorney, was in the room when the students spoke out. Is such an attitude widespread? she was asked. "I run into it everywhere I go," Mrs. Martin said. "And I say this as one who believes in integration as our only hope."

The distress and ambiguity on the part of the Negro students was perhaps indicative of the entire black community in white America as the nation seemed destined for continued periods of divisive and possibly disruptive race relations. Roy Innis, the national director of the Congress of Racial Equality, was traveling the South seeking to set up separate school districts for black and white. Negro legislators in Michigan voted against a plan submitted by the Detroit school board to vastly increase the integration in the public schools, holding out instead for more community control that would free predominantly black schools from "white rule." Negro students in colleges across the nation were demanding separate dormitories and departments and courses in black studies. Several black nationalist groups in the Northern cities were working for the day when blacks would own their own enclaves in America. Some were seeking entire states. Floyd McKissick, the former civil rights leader, was head of a group planning to construct an all-black community in North Carolina called Soul City.

On the other hand, thousands of Negro parents were continuing to press school integration suits, in Northern cities as well as Southern ones. The largest and most stable of the Negro organizations, the National Association for the Advancement of Colored People, was committed to integration to the point of openly opposing Negroes who sought separatism. Charles Evers, the first Negro to be elected mayor of a biracial municipality in Mississippi since Reconstruction, was trying to make Fayette, Mississippi, a community where both blacks and whites would want to live and work. Fayette and the surrounding counties with predominantly Negro populations could easily become a political and economic base for the black nationalist movement, but Evers was convinced that only in the sharing of power and wealth was there a viable future for blacks, and for all of America. In Philadelphia, Chicago, and other Northern cities, black community groups advocating radical changes in the American system were reaching out for coalitions with poor whites.

All this prompted many whites to ask, as they have many times in the past, "What do *they* want?"

It is no longer sufficient, if it ever was, to say that Negro Americans want what white Americans want, especially now that there is an abundance of evidence that many white Americans do not know what they want. There is ambivalence in the Negro community and as many shades of political and philosophical opinions among blacks as among whites. The picture is further confused by the fact that the public utterances, frequently intended for tactical advantage, may not match long-range goals. Indeed, black leaders have written that there is within the individual constantly warring feelings as a result of being at once both a member of a frequently despised minority and an American with all the promises and obligations that entails. In 1897, W. E. B. DuBois defined the dilemma in a speech delivered in Washington: "What, after all, am I? Am I an American or a Negro? Can I be both? Or is it my duty to cease to be a Negro as soon as possible and be an American?"

The difficulty of defining what Negroes want is pointed up

by a dilemma facing department stores having both white and Negro customers in the summer of 1971—whether to have a black Santa Claus for the Christmas season. An executive for a chain of stores in a large Northern city, himself a Negro, said there were at least three points of view among Negro customers. First, there were those who wanted a black Santa for their children in the belief that the traditional white Santa fosters white paternalism while a black Santa enhances black pride and self-dependence. Second, numbers of Negroes have come to reject the idea of a Santa Claus of any race on the ground that he is part of the white institutions that have kept black people oppressed. Third, many Negroes find nothing wrong with a white Santa and would object to having biracial Santas in a store because they would foster segregation—the white children lining up for the white Santa and the Negro children for the black Santa. (White attitudes, of course, also were a part of the problem.) The executive said the attitudes might vary from city to city and the issue was such a delicate one he would advise opinion surveys of customers before making a decision.

Yet the subject of Negro goals may not be as opaque and complex as the white misunderstandings of what it is all about. Historically, the movement on behalf of black separatism has ebbed and flowed in almost direct proportion to the extent of white hostility to blacks. At times when the white society displayed some willingness to open institutions and political processes to Negroes, the separatist movement was least in evidence. At times when it appeared that whites were becoming more unreceptive to black participation and equality, separatism made gains in the black community. In recent years, it has been made clear time and again that the majority of blacks do not counsel violent overthrow of the govern-

7

ment, back-to-Africa movements, or the creation of states on the basis of race. Violence, when it became a tactic in the Negro revolution in the 1960's, was used to demonstrate injustice and discontent rather than to bring down the society. Essentially, the center of the Negro movement has been and continues to be conservative and optimistic, especially when placed alongside the New Left movement of whites. The great majority of Negroes have made it clear they want a part of the American system. But this does not mean that they do not see its imperfections and would not favor radical change. The findings of opinion polls, interviews with scores of Negro leaders of various political persuasions, and the writings of black authors make it plain that blacks view the American promise of liberty and justice for all with a much colder eye than the mass of white citizens. For to them, more than a century after emancipation, the creed that has sustained several generations of whites remains to be fulfilled.

In order to understand current attitudes and trends, it is helpful to know something of the black nationalist movements of the past. They have all been characterized, as are the current ones, by the belief that blacks have a common heritage and culture distinct from those of other peoples and that in order to prosper and retain the positive aspects of their society they should rule themselves and decide their own future. They have sought withdrawal, both politically and physically, into their own communities. This has ranged from efforts to return en masse to Africa to establishment of autonomous black neighborhoods. Blacks have identified with their African origins and their history of suffering and struggle to overcome white oppression. They have proceeded from the assumption that white Americans would never recognize their potential and their right to be treated with justice and equality.

Black nationalist movements sprang up in this country almost from the moment that blacks were in a position to organize. In 1787, for example, shortly after Massachusetts became a free state, a group of about eighty free Negroes in Boston petitioned the state government for assistance in moving to Africa. Nothing ever came of their movement. But Paul Cuffee, a black ship captain operating out of Massachusetts, promoted the idea of opening trade between the United States and West Africa so as to permit free blacks to return to the country of their origin. The War of 1812 delayed his plans and he died in 1817 after seeing one shipload of settlers land in Sierra Leone. But his efforts to persuade both whites and free blacks of the advantages of a back-to-Africa movement led to founding of the American Colonization Society, a largely white organization that endured into the twentieth century. During its lifetime, the society transported thousands of blacks to Liberia, which it founded, and provided the basis for the Negro-led colonization movements that sprang up around the turn of the century.

It was not until about 1890, after it had become clear that the nation had agreed to the South's methods of dealing with the former slaves, that the black nationalist movements gained a strong foothold among the mass of Negroes. After the Civil War, the country spent three decades deciding what role the Negro minority would play in national life. Bit by bit, the views of the South came to be accepted and incorporated in government and private institutions. In 1876, Reconstruction was ended and power restored to Southern whites. In the years following, Negroes were systematically disfranchised, lynchings and other violence against blacks mounted, the Southern states enacted volumes of segregation laws and constitutions that for the next half century would relegate Negroes to second-class citizenship.

The Supreme Court in a series of decisions struck down the Civil Rights Act of 1875 and in general diminished the federal presence in Southern race relations; and in 1896 the court ruled in *Plessy vs. Ferguson* that "separate but equal" public schools were constitutional, giving legal sanction to the entire mass of segregation laws. The idea of white racial superiority was in vogue in the Western world and made considerable inroads in American intellectual thought. National journals such as *Harper's, Scribner's* and *The Atlantic* joined the South in romanticizing slavery and depicting the Negro as a foot-shuffling, comic stereotype. Both Northern and Southern newspapers fed the trend to anti-Negro violence by reporting the victims of lynchings guilty of whatever atrocities they may have been accused. It became clear by the 1890's that Negroes, who still lived largely in the South, were intended from the national point of view to remain dependent on whites, politically powerless, and a people apart.

In addition to the loss of those civil rights that had been promised by both the Civil War and Reconstruction, the economic depressions late in the century left much of the rural laboring class destitute and helped create an ideal climate for the rise of black nationalism. This movement, in all of its various forms, probably had more followers than was generally acknowledged at the time because it was obscured by other movements led by the best-known Negro leaders of the period, Booker T. Washington and W. E. B. DuBois.

Washington, the founder of Tuskegee Institute in Alabama, aware of the wide gulf that separated blacks from whites, accepted for the short run the segregation, inequality, and disfranchisement then being imposed by white society and advised his followers to learn a trade or vocation, work hard, and accumulate wealth. Eventually, he said, Negroes would be accepted by acquiring the values honored by white America.

DuBois advocated a different approach. An intellectual with degrees from Harvard and Berlin and operating from a Northern base, DuBois said that the oppression by whites should not be accepted for any length of time, and he set about organizing protests. But his differences with Washington were ones of means, not ends. Both wanted acceptance by the white majority and both believed that this was ultimately possible. DuBois put much faith in the building of a Negro elite, "the talented tenth," which would be highly educated and articulate and thus would be able to bridge the gap between blacks and whites. Both leaders enjoyed the support of wealthy and influential whites.

The similarities between the Washington and DuBois movements were defined by Edwin S. Redkey in *Black Exodus,* a study of the black nationalist movements from 1890 to 1910, published in 1969. "Each ideology expected a black elite to win the dignity sought by all Afro-Americans," Redkey wrote. "Both factions believed that once the elite had led the way, upper-class American attitudes would change and the lower classes of whites would imitate their betters and overcome their prejudice against blacks. Each alternative was primarily a middle-class plan and reflected the middle-class optimism of American culture."

Redkey pointed out that the black nationalist movements had their base largely among poor blacks because neither the gospel of black wealth nor that of black talent could help the tenant farmer "who had neither money, education nor faith in America." By 1890 a significant portion of the Negro population had lost the basic optimism in America shared by Washington and DuBois.

The chief leader and advocate of black separatism during this period was Henry McNeal Turner, a man of considerable talent and ambition whose efforts to achieve his potential within the white-dominated institutions had been frustrated at every turn. Turner was free born in South Carolina in 1834. Apprenticed to work beside slaves in the cotton fields, he ran away and found a job sweeping floors in a law office. There young law clerks, impressed by his abilities, secretly taught him to read and write. At the age of twenty, Turner was ordained a traveling evangelist in the Southern Methodist church, which at that time had both white and Negro members but was, of course, run exclusively by whites. He traveled the South, preaching to people of both races.

But the prejudices he encountered caused him to join the Negro-governed African Methodist Episcopal (A.M.E.) church, in which he later became a bishop. During the Civil War, he was assigned a church in Washington, D. C., where he became a leader in recruiting black troops for the Union armies. After the war, he was a chaplain in the Freedman's Bureau, the government agency formed to help the newly freed slaves, and was assigned to Georgia. But even in that organization he found unbearable the prejudices against him because of his race. He soon resigned and set about organizing A.M.E. churches in Georgia. At the same time, he became a leader in Republican state politics and was elected to the 1867 Georgia Constitutional Convention and the 1867 legislature.

Government and politics, Turner believed, offered an opportunity for Negroes to share power with whites. But it was not long before the state government disqualified blacks from holding elective office and Turner, of course, was cast out. He was appointed postmaster at Macon, Georgia, but after serving only two weeks was dismissed under false charges of fraud, counterfeiting, and theft. By this time, Turner had become convinced that separatism was the only recourse for Negroes. His speeches and writing on the futility of finding an accommodation with whites contained a theme that was to be revived by black power advocates of the 1960's. "White men are not to be trusted," Bishop Turner said seventy years before Stokely Carmichael said, "I've never known a white man I could trust."

After the Supreme Court declared the Civil Rights Act of 1875 to be unconstitutional, Turner said that Negroes no longer owed allegiance to the government. The Constitution, he said, was now a "dirty rag, a cheat, a libel and ought to be spit upon by every Negro in the land." In a burst of black anger, Turner said if the decision should be accepted by the country (which it was) Negroes should "prepare to return to Africa or get ready for extermination."

Thereafter, Turner devoted most of his time and energies to promoting back-to-Africa movements. As was to be expected, he encountered bitter opposition from blacks who sought integration into the white society. And he found himself frequently in coalition with the most conservative and anti-Negro whites, those who wanted to be rid of blacks. These strange alliances were to recur in later years whenever black separatist movements were organized.

Bishop Turner's movement was a failure, at least in terms of the numbers transported to Africa and in the extent of disappointment among those who subscribed to it. His own schemes, built on the American Emigration Society's experiences, resulted in only two shiploads of blacks being transported to Liberia, in the 1890's. And the majority of those several hundred emigrants found only poverty, hardship, and disease upon their arrival. Other emigration movements fared even worse, and the newspapers of the day carried stories of poor blacks being bilked of their money by fraudulant emigration schemes and of Negroes arriving penniless in New York and other port cities to find that the anticipated transportation to Africa was nonexistent.

The middle-class blacks of the day never subscribed to the emigration movement, even when they were in agreement with Turner about the injustices and oppression of the white society. It was their beliefs that attracted the most public attention. Nevertheless, the movement for a separate black society seemed to have had considerable support among poor blacks who saw no chance of sharing in the American dream.

"Just how broad the movement was is difficult to judge with precision," Redkey wrote, "but signs of emigrationism appeared in all the deep South and Southwestern states, where the vast majority of Afro-Americans lived. Thousands were caught up directly in one or more of the emigration schemes and millions may have shared the black nationalists' pessimism about the United States."

There were movements for blacks to settle in South America, Mexico, and even Canada, none of which reached fruition. But during the period, a number of all-black communities were settled across the South and Southwest. Edwin P. McCabe, a Negro politician from Kansas, attempted to establish a black state, Oklahoma, which was opened to homestead settlement in the 1890's. He planned for a voting majority of blacks to settle in each electoral district of the new territory and he hoped that he would be appointed the first governor. Thousands of blacks responded. More than seven thousand entered the territory during the first year of settlement and a number of all-black towns were established. But whites also came and were soon taking steps to stem the influx of blacks. Even in all-black Langston City there were reports of whites entering and attempting to frighten the Negroes away. The Choctaw Indians also were resentful of the Negroes. Many of the black homesteaders soon became disillusioned and began seeking land elsewhere. Oklahoma thus became a center of the back-to-Africa movement.

Some of the black towns established during that period remain to this day in areas across the South. They may have provided a degree of relief from white oppression but they did not bring the kind of freedom and prosperity that their founders envisioned. Some are monuments to poverty and stagnation, to the emptiness of the first significant black separatist movements in this country. Bishop Turner's crusade was based too much on the negative aspect of simply escaping from oppression. As Redkey pointed out, it lacked both the intellectual leadership indispensable for a successful nationalist movement and a positive cultural and economic base. It was built on an "Africanized American dream," Redkey wrote, and thus could not stand on its own.

In any event, those black leaders who counseled working within the white society in the belief that Negroes could gain acceptance by either protest or accommodation prevailed over the advocates of separatism, and they did so with substantial white support. But the nation did not respond as both Washington and DuBois had hoped. The "Southern solution" continued in favor well into the twentieth century, and black nationalism again came into vogue among the poor and oppressed.

The period was following World War I and the leader was Marcus Garvey, who developed a spectacular following within a very short time. By the time Garvey burst upon the scene, significant changes had taken place among American Negroes. The migration of blacks from the farms of the South to the Northern cities, a trend that was to continue for most of the century, had begun. Millions of Negroes had fought in the war or worked in defense plants and were little inclined to return to the lives they had known before. The protest movement started by DuBois had grown considerably and a body of black writers and intellectuals had emerged. At the same time, however, a new wave of oppression against blacks was sweeping the land. New waves of lynchings broke out. Race riots occurred in a number of cities, the largest in Chicago in 1919, lasting eleven days and resulting in thirty-six deaths and more than five hundred injuries. These took the form not of the black rampages of the 1960's but of bands of blacks and whites warring against each other. The Ku Klux Klan was undergoing a tremendous revival. The country was experiencing a Communist scare and Negro leaders such as DuBois were accused of being part of a "red conspiracy."

Garvey was born in Jamaica in 1887 and came to the United States in 1916, a year after Bishop Turner died. He called himself "Provisional President of Africa" and he sought support for a black empire that was to be governed by black men. Establishing himself in Harlem, he founded the Universal Negro Improvement Association and its newspaper, *The Negro World*. Like Turner, he preached of the glories of Africa. He declared he would organize 400 million Negroes "to draw up the banner of democracy on the continent of Africa." A dark, heavyset man with tremendous energy, a dynamic personal presence, an exceptional talent for public relations, and a master of phrase-making, Garvey dressed his followers in brilliant uniforms. They paraded under such banners as the Universal African Motor Corps, the Black Eagle Flying Corps, and the Universal Black Cross Nurses. Garvey established orders of nobility such as the Knights of the Distinguished Order of Ethiopia and the Duke of Uganda.

The extent of active membership in the Garvey organization is difficult to establish but there can be no doubt that large numbers were involved. In 1920, an estimated 25,000 members assembled in New York for a thirty-day convention of the UNIA and the dues and contributions poured in by the millions of dollars. With money collected from his followers, Garvey established businesses and bought three ships which he planned to operate as the Black Star Steamship Line. His plan was identical to that of Paul Cuffee, the Negro ship captain, in the early 1800's. The ship would be used for both commerce between the United States and African ports and for transportation of Negro colonists to Africa.

In this and many other ways, Garvey appealed to race pride. "We have died for five hundred years for an alien race," he thundered. "The time has come for the Negro to die for himself." DuBois and other Negro intellectuals reacted to Garvey's movement with scorn and disbelief. But they could not ignore him, for he had a massive following. His appeal, like Turner's, was to the poor blacks. But where Turner had to reach people scattered in rural areas across the South and Southwest, Garvey was able to organize the same

17

class of people who were by then crowded into urban areas. Thus it was much easier to get a mass movement organized. By 1919, Garvey claimed to have established forty-one chapters of the UNIA in the United States and elsewhere, and in 1922 he said the membership included two million Negro Americans.

But Garvey's grand plan never materialized. His great organizing skill did not extend to business management. In 1923, he was convicted of mail fraud and sentenced to five years in prison. He tried to direct his movement from his jail cell in Atlanta, but without success. His movement evaporated faster than it had come into being. In 1927, Garvey was pardoned by President Coolidge and deported to Jamaica. He died penniless in 1940.

For all its emptiness and false assumptions, however, the Garvey movement pointed up the extent of discontent among the masses of Negroes. Saunders Redding, in a history of the American Negro, *They Came in Chains*, wrote:

> The Garvey Movement cannot be dismissed merely as the aberration of an organized pressure group. The least that can be said of it is that it was an authentic folk movement. Its spirit of race chauvinism had the sympathy of the overwhelming majority of the Negro people, including those who opposed its objectives.

In succeeding years, nevertheless, black nationalism declined as the tactics of organized protest against white injustices and oppression became increasingly popular and effective. During the height of the great civil rights movement of the 1950's and 1960's, which succeeded in eliminating the legal barriers to equality and making considerable changes in white attitudes, black separatist organizations were functioning but they were generally considered an infinitesimal part of the Negro community and irrelevant to the changes that were taking place in America. It was not until the civil rights movement had reached its peak and new storm clouds were on the horizon in race relations that leaders who had been at the forefront of the nonviolent rights drive began talking of Garvey and the need of blacks to form separate enclaves. It is important to know why this was so.

2

The Rise and Fall of Nonviolence

ONE DECEMBER evening in 1955 a department store seamstress in Montgomery, Alabama, had sore feet. Those sore feet were the catalyst of the most remarkable era in the history of Negro Americans. Mrs. Rose Parks caught the bus for her home after work as usual. Montgomery, like most cities throughout the South, had all manner of segregation ordinances that regulated the eating, sleeping, riding, sitting, learning, and recreation habits of blacks. On buses operated in the city, Negroes were required to sit in the back or in a "neutral" zone in the middle, so long as no white passenger required the "neutral" seats. Mrs. Parks took a seat in the neutral zone, but after a few blocks white passengers boarded and, as usual, demanded seats. Mrs. Parks refused to move, not out of planned protest, though she was a member of the NAACP. "My feet hurt," she explained later.

The driver stopped the bus and called the police. Mrs. Parks was arrested and taken to jail. When word of the arrest spread through the Negro community, a city-wide boycott of the bus line was organized. One of the leaders was the Reverend Dr. Martin Luther King, Jr., a young Baptist minister who had grown up in Atlanta, earned a doctorate at Boston University and was deeply influenced by the philosophy and leadership of Mohandas K. Ghandi. King believed that the technique of nonviolent protest that Ghandi had used in gaining freedom for India could be employed successfully by American Negroes, and this was what happened in Montgomery.

The black community organized car pools to take people to and from work, a means of bringing economic pressure on the bus company. Mass meetings were held regularly in which the particpants were instructed in the nonviolent technique. Although some Negroes lost their jobs because of the boycott, violence and harassment was used against others, and the leaders were arrested under state charges of plotting to bankrupt the bus company, the mass of Negroes refrained from a violent response and strengthened their commitment to the boycott. The strike, which lasted a year, received widespread attention in the United States and elsewhere. The Supreme Court struck down the law under which Mrs. Parks had been arrested and ordered Montgomery's buses desegregated. On the morning of December 21, 1956, Dr. King and other Negro leaders rode triumphantly on an integrated bus.

The nonviolent movement in which many thousands were involved in protests against laws and policies considered unjust was to last a decade and bring more fundamental changes than any other of the Negro movements. It was used in towns and cities across the South and even to some extent in Northern cities to combat segregation practiced by law, policy or custom in education, transportation and public accommodations, and many other forms of discrimination. The movement brought enactment of the Omnibus Civil

Rights Act of 1964, the most far-reaching document in behalf of Negro rights since the Emancipation Proclamation, and the Voting Rights Act of 1965, which added more than one million Negroes to the voting rolls in the South. Further, the nonviolent movement brought enormous gains in respect and dignity for blacks and it inspired other minorities and groups, from American Indians to ethnic whites, to organize protests against various forms of discrimination.

One reason nonviolence could succeed for Negroes was that by the time it came into being the American government and other institutions were at last beginning to respond to the needs of black people. During the 1930's the Democratic Party in its rise to dominance in American politics began to appeal to blacks as one element of a coalition that would include organized labor, intellectuals, white ethnic groups, and, strangely, Southern whites. President Roosevelt appointed Negroes to prominent positions in the government and during World War II instituted, in response to Negro pressures, a fair employment practices commission that opened many defense jobs to blacks. After the war, President Truman continued the Roosevelt policies and all the while the Supreme Court, under the influence of men appointed by Roosevelt and Truman, was turning from a conservative, pro-business body into one that emphasized individual liberties and civil rights.

In the black community, the back-to-Africa movements of Turner and Garvey were all but forgotten, as was Washington's policy of accommodation to the white system. The dominant Negro protest movement, led chiefly by the NAACP, emphasized integration, so much so that it chose to put desegregation of schools ahead of other such basic needs as voter registration. And integration was endemic to the nonviolent movement. For one of the essentials of nonviolence as taught by Dr. King and other leaders was that it was concerned not simply with the well-being of blacks but with the condition of society as a whole. Dr. King and his nonviolent armies were committed to freeing the oppressor, as well as the oppressed, from his special kind of burden. In this, nonviolence was markedly different from the black nationalist movements that came before and afterward.

It is difficult to overstate the extent of change that nonviolence effected in the basic laws under which millions of Negroes had lived. The segregation statutes and others designed to keep blacks a people apart were thoroughly laced in the social fabric of the Southern and border states, so that generations of blacks and whites born under them grew up thinking the laws commanded the natural and proper order of society. When Mrs. Parks refused to move from her seat on that December evening of 1955, this phalanx of legal requirements was still in force, even though the Supreme Court had made a start in striking it down. It would be naïve even to imagine that the courts and the national government would have succeeded in rooting out the entrenched legal system of segregation without the nonviolent movement and its impact on public opinion. By 1965, the body of law put together after Reconstruction and strengthened for decades was gone, even if the attitudes of many had not been changed in the process.

The practical effect could be seen in many ways and many places. Clarendon County, South Carolina, provided an example, almost a caricature of the Old South. The county had a plantation economy with thousands of Negroes, first under slavery and later under the system of caste, working its black fertile fields. Negroes vastly outnumbered whites and consequently their lives were ruled by the old mores of exclusion and violence. The Clarendon County school system was one of the parties directed to desegregate in the landmark Supreme Court decision of 1954, *Brown* vs. *Board of Education of Topeka.* Even by 1969, the Clarendon County schools had not fully complied with the decision but the county, nevertheless, had undergone a transformation.

On May 15 of that year, the fifteenth anniversary of *Brown,* Billie Fleming, a NAACP leader who had been at the forefront of the South Carolina rights movement for many years, sat behind his desk at the funeral home he operates and reminisced about how life had been and reflected on the future. He deplored the long delay in completing desegregation of the schools and complained of other problems that Negroes were encountering, but in the end he said:

"You know many of our people have gone to live in Northern cities. They left to find jobs and to get away from the vicious oppression that we suffered here. Well, they come back from time to time, when there is a death in the family, and they talk to me about it. Many of them see the difference here now. They say they would like to come back to live if they could find employment.

"What is the difference? For one thing, we do not live under the threat of violence as we did. The whites know they can no longer get away with it. We can get on a bus without having to take a back seat. We don't have 'white only' signs facing us everywhere we go. We have got a movement going. Our people are voting now in greater numbers, and we are going to keep the pressure on. We have got some antipoverty money from Washington. It is not enough, but it is a start. The thing is, people *can* live here now with some freedom if they can find a job, and if they can it is better than being in the Northern ghettos."

Gunnar Myrdal, the Swedish economist and sociologist, whose work on the race problem in the United States, *The American Dilemma*, had an important influence in the civil rights movement, paid one of his periodic visits to the United States in 1969. Asked by a reporter to reassess the racial situation in light of all that had happened since his book was published in the early 1940's, Myrdal said he frequently encountered people who said there had been little change in social conditions as they affect black people. "I say there has been enormous change," he said. "Many today do not know how bad it was then." In many areas of the South, he explained, Negroes were used in almost the same way they had been under slavery.

Of course there had been no magic change in attitudes, and the violence of the 1960's and the mass movement of whites into exclusive white suburbs had in many ways increased racial antagonisms. But the discrimination that remained was extralegal and in violation of national policy and of the new body of civil rights law that replaced the vast array of segregation statutes. This was the change brought about by the nonviolent movement. More than any other force in American history, nonviolence raised the standing of black people within the society and dispelled the myth that Negroes were content in a position of servitude. It succeeded partly because it contained both protest and persuasion and always embodied the American creed of liberty and justice for all.

After the Montgomery bus boycott, the nonviolent crusades led by Dr. King and others fell into a pattern. In a community where Negroes felt they had been subjected to

25

particular injustices a protest movement would be organized. Mass meetings would be held, usually in churches, and those attending would be inspired to participate through song and oratory detailing the grievances. Street marches and other demonstrations would be held daily, and at crucial periods during the campaign the participants would break the laws or policy they considered unjust. This might include sit-ins at segregated lunch counters, marches in violation of regulations or refusal to leave voter registration offices where blacks were subjected to discrimination.

The theory was to plague the community—"lovingly," as Dr. King said—until discriminatory practices were ended. This was done by filling up the jails, putting a burden on the law enforcement body and the courts, and appealing to the conscience of the nation by showing thousands of people out in the streets exposing themselves to violence and arrest to achieve equal treatment. Some of the crusades failed for lack of support in the black community, or for inability to attract national attention and sympathy or because of unrelenting control of the community by white leaders. Albany, Georgia, where thousands went to jail but achieved little change was an example of failure. But in a number of other communities the crusades succeeded remarkably, both locally and nationally.

In such varied cities as Orangeburg, South Carolina; Jackson, Mississippi; Danville, Virginia; Cambridge, Maryland; and Pine Bluff, Arkansas, the authorities made some concessions to the Negro crusades. And there were changes effected even in cities where there were no well-organized crusades. During his St. Augustine, Florida, campaign in 1964, Dr. King said the movement was bringing "intangible results outside the community where it is carried out. There is a hardening of attitudes in situations like this one [St. Augustine]. But other cities see and say, 'We don't want to be another Albany or another Birmingham,' and they make changes. Some communities, like this one, have to bear the cross."

As was pointed out earlier, some of the crusades had direct, positive results. When Negro demonstrators were confronted by firehoses and police dogs in Birmingham in 1963, the Kennedy Administration drafted the Omnibus Civil Rights Act, which was enacted the following year as the nonviolent crusades spread to scores of cities. The rationale the administration gave for proposing such a broad statute was that it would take the dispute out of the streets and into the courts—an effort to be rid of the plague that the nonviolent armies were bringing on the land. Under the terms of the law, the national government was charged with moving against discrimination in employment, education, government services, public accommodations, and every area in which federal monies were used. The Selma campaign in 1965 brought a much stronger Voting Rights Act than the Johnson Administration had dreamed of prior to the great marches and confrontations in central Alabama and elsewhere across the nation.

There are many degrees of racial integration, and these will be discussed later in an effort to define the role most Negroes wish to play in American life. The nonviolent movement stood not only for removing the racial barriers that in themselves represented an affront to all black people but for a free mingling of the races in almost all areas of society. The movement itself was thoroughly integrated and one of its cardinal rules was that it was open and free to everyone. Whites played an important role in the movement. They provided a large share of the money needed to keep it going.

White volunteers—ministers, students, lawyers, house-wives—worked in the freedom houses, participated in the marches, sit-ins, and mass meetings and went to jail along with blacks.

The theme song of the movement was "We Shall Over-come" and one verse sung over and over across the land went, "Black and white together/Black and white toge-ther/We shall overcome, some day." Dr. King and his fol-lowers were adamant against segregation in any form. In his letter from the Birmingham jail, written in 1963 to white clergymen who had declared that his leading of a demonstra-tion in violation of an injunction was "unwise and untimely," Dr. King wrote:

All segregation statutes are unjust because segregation distorts the soul and damages the personality. It gives the segregator a false sense of superiority and the segregated a false sense of inferiority. Segregation, to use the terminology of the Jewish philosopher Mar-tin Buber, substitutes an "I-it" relationship for an "I-thou" rela-tionship and ends up relegating persons to the status of things. Hence segregation is not only politically, economically and socio-logically unsound, it is morally wrong and sinful. Paul Tillich has said that sin is separation. Is not segregation an existential expres-sion of man's tragic separation, his awful estrangement, his terrible sinfulness?

In a book entitled *Why We Can't Wait*, written early in 1964, Dr. King expressed the belief that the movement would help poor whites, who shared much of the poverty and degredation known to blacks, and the entire society as well:

Just as a doctor will occasionally reopen a wound, because a dangerous infection hovers beneath the half-healed surface, the revolution for human rights is opening up unhealthy areas in American life and permitting a new and wholesome healing to take place. Eventually the civil rights movement will have contributed infinitely more to the nation than the eradication of racial injustice. It will have enlarged the concept of brotherhood to a vision of total interrelatedness. On that day, Canon John Donne's doctrine, "no man is an islande," will find its truest application in the United States.

All of the major civil rights organizations subscribed to this belief in those days—the Student Nonviolent Coordinating Committee (which Dr. King had helped found), the Congress of Racial Equality, as well as the old-line organizations such as the NAACP and the National Urban League and hosts of local Negro groups. The tactic was moral suasion combined with organized protest and an appeal to basic tenets in American history and tradition. Masses of whites were touched by the cause. The United States had never seen anything like the nonviolent movement.

Yet the movement had its limitations, which soon became evident. It was rarely effective on the local level outside the South. In that region the religious beliefs and traditions, which most Negroes shared, sustained the kind of dedication and self-sacrifice needed for large-scale nonviolent actions. In virtually every community, the movement was organized around the church. And hope and the spirit of redemptive love was always present.

In the Northern cities, where blacks had settled in large numbers, the Negro areas were split into so many diverse factions that it was difficult to get any kind of mass movement started, and the religious tradition was not nearly as strong and viable as in the South. In the North, and later in the South as well, the targets of the movement were less visible. Discrimination was more subtle and had rarely been protected by law. The big cities were impersonal and unresponsive. When Dr. King attempted to organize a crusade in Chicago built around the need for better and integrated housing in 1966, Mayor Richard J. Daley welcomed him with open arms, but nothing happened. The vast city simply swallowed up the crusade and went on as before. From there the Southern Christian Leadership Conference that Dr. King headed went into decline and there were no more massive nonviolent campaigns attracting national attention and the sympathy of national audiences.

Even in the South, nonviolence lost much of its effectiveness. The national laws and Supreme Court rulings of the period succeeded in removing most of the legal barriers that the movement was directed against. And Southern officials learned that the movement would only be strengthened by offering the kind of blatant opposition that Sheriff James Clark of Selma and Police Chief Eugene (Bull) Connor of Birmingham had symbolized. Many who had worked in the movement left it to protest the war in Vietnam, which began in 1965 to cut deeply into domestic programs that were vital to poor blacks.

Throughout the nation, the kind of freedom, equality, and opportunity that Dr. King and others had sought for Negroes remained a long way from realization. Negroes had not secured those rights promised by the new laws and policy, and almost everyone agreed that further organization and leadership were needed to complete what the movement had started. But the nonviolent movement was not able to fill that need. In an important sense it was abandoned before it could be strengthened and put to the test under changed circumstances. Many who had subscribed to its beliefs were in pursuit of other philosophies that set entirely different goals and ambitions for black America.

3

The Emergence of "~~Black Power~~"

U.W.P.

AT THE HEIGHT of the nonviolent movement, black nationalism was rising again in the Northern cities from the ruins of the Turner and Garvey movements and from various organizations embodying similar teachings. It had never died but had for so long been dormant and overshadowed by the ferment and excitement of the drive for integration that many leaders, both black and white, were somewhat surprised and alarmed when, in the late 1950's and early 1960's, the Black Muslims began attracting considerable support with another variation of separatism. One of the key slogans, "There is no white man a Muslim can trust," was an echo of Bishop Turner.

In his letter from the Birmingham jail in 1963, Dr. King drew this perspective of what was taking place among blacks:

I stand in the middle of two opposing forces in the Negro community. One is a force of complacency, made up in part of Negroes who, as a result of long years of oppression, are so drained of self-respect and a sense of "somebodiness" that they have adjusted to segregation; and in part of a few middle-class Negroes

31

who, because of a degree of academic and economic security and because in some ways they profit by segregation, have become insensitive to the problems of the masses. The other force is one of bitterness and hatred, and it comes perilously close to advocating violence. It is expressed in the various black nationalist groups that are springing up across the nation, the largest and best known being Elijah Muhammad's Muslim movement. Nourished by the Negro's frustration over the continued existence of racial discrimination, this movement is made up of people who have lost faith in America, who have absolutely repudiated Christianity, and who have concluded that the white man is an incorrigible "devil." I have tried to stand between these two forces, saying that we need emulate neither the "do-nothingism" of the complacent nor the hatred and despair of the black nationalist.

If the nonviolent movement was scoring successes, why then was black nationalism on the rise? The answer lies in the explanation as to why Dr. King's Chicago crusade failed. The gains achieved through nonviolence were registered largely in the South. The migration to Northern cities had been going on for decades and even as Congress enacted the great civil rights legislation of the 1960's, life for millions of blacks in the large cities was becoming increasingly difficult and isolated from the economic gains that most white Americans were making. In good times and bad, the movement of Negroes to the city slums had continued. As mechanization and mass production on the farms replaced sharecroppers and the family farm, the Negro family would move to the city where there was some promise of employment. But there was little to offer in the way of employment for people without education or training in the cities. The family would go on welfare, the males would drift away and be drawn into crime and delinquency.

By 1950, the jobs in unskilled labor that had sustained other immigrant minorities had given way to mechanization. The trade unions, which had provided a ladder upward for countless white poor, were closed to blacks. The inner cities where the Negroes lived were becoming more and more economically depressed as the whites moved to outlying areas and took much of the economy with them. President Johnson, in an address at Howard University in June, 1965, stated something of the problem in his appeal to whites to have an "understanding heart" and help blacks escape the cycle of poverty and deprivation. Thirty-five years earlier, he noted, the unemployment rate for Negroes and whites was about the same. By 1965, the Negro rate was twice as high. The unemployment rate for Negro teen-age boys was 23 percent, as compared to 13 percent for whites. Between 1955 and 1957, 22 percent of experienced Negro workers were without jobs at some time during the year. Between 1961 and 1963, that proportion had risen to 29 percent. And so on.

During most of the country's history, attention had been focused on discrimination in the South, where it was by far the greatest and made dramatic by the Gothic hates and guilts that prevailed in that region. But the South had no monopoly on barring blacks. Northern Negroes had only to witness a Mayor Orville Hubbard of Dearborn who made his city a white enclave unsafe for black inhabitants or the violence turned against a black family when it moved into a white neighborhood to see the extent of exclusion.

"There is general agreement among American Negroes," C. Eric Lincoln wrote in 1961 in *The Black Muslims in America*, "that the white man has failed to demonstrate any real capacity for genuine brotherhood and equal justice.

There is a widespread belief that the white man will *never* of his own accord accept nonwhites as his equals in status and opportunity, in America or elsewhere."

The same year, James Baldwin wrote in *The New York Times Magazine* of the frustrations of Negroes living where equality is publicly preached but little heeded. "Northerners proffer their indignation about the South as a kind of badge, as proof of good intentions," he wrote. "They never suspect that they thus increase, in the heart of the Negro they address, a kind of helpless pain and rage—and pity. Negroes know how little most white people are prepared to implement their words with deeds, how little, when the chips are down, they are prepared to risk."

There were other reasons for the renewed interest in black nationalism. The winds of change were beginning to sweep through Africa and blacks there were seeking independence. American Negroes identified with that movement and, as Lincoln wrote, "are horrified to know that they may soon be the only victims of racial subordination left in the civilized world."

And the Negro protests that were under way in the South, along with the bitter resistance to change shown by whites, inspired Northern Negroes into activism of one form or another. Many of the poor blacks in the Northern slums favored black nationalism, just as they had under Bishop Turner and Marcus Garvey. When the Black Muslims began organizing, in Detroit in the 1930's, a survey of the membership showed it to be made up predominantly of poor blacks who had recently migrated from the South. And it was the poor who made up the bulk of the scores of thousands in the Muslims in the early 1960's.

Lincoln, in his study of the Muslims, told of a play that

the organization staged in major cities across the country. In it, a black prosecutor stood before a black jury, pointed to a white man who cringed in the defendant's chair, and read an indictment on behalf of the Black Nation of Islam:

I charge the white man with being the greatest liar on earth! I charge the white man with being the greatest drunkard on earth. . . . I charge the white man with being the greatest gambler on earth. I charge the white man, ladies and gentlemen of the jury, with being the greatest peace-breaker on earth. I charge the white man with being the greatest adulterer on earth. I charge the white man with being the greatest robber on earth. I charge the white man with being the greatest deceiver on earth. I charge the white man with being the greatest trouble-maker on earth. So, therefore, ladies and gentlemen of the jury, I ask you, bring back a verdict of guilty as charged.

The foreman polled the jury and within seconds read the verdict: "Guilty as charged." The sentence was "death" and the defendant was dragged away, protesting his innocence and declaring all he had done for "the Nigra people." The audience roared in approval and brought the players back for several curtain calls.

The condemnation of whites as evil and the belief that blacks of the world would some day prevail over them was one of the chief appeals of the Muslims. They demanded the absolute separation of black and white races. The return to Africa that Garvey and Turner had advocated was considered impractical. They sought instead their own land on which to build their own society. In the interim they acquired considerable real estate holdings, businesses, schools, hospitals, and community centers. Founded on a religious base, the Muslims in many respects offered positive outlets for black frustrations. Their converts in many instances were pimps, hustlers, and dope addicts who were led into new, constructive lives. The Muslim society was based on morality, honesty, hard work, and clean living. And their cause was effectively and widely publicized by a brilliant Harlem minister, Malcolm X, who enunciated the cause of urban blacks better than anyone had ever done before.

In his autobiography, published after his assassination in 1965, Malcolm explained that, unlike most Negro groups, the Muslims cared little whether Lyndon Johnson or Barry Goldwater were elected President in 1964. "If it had been Goldwater," he wrote, "black people would at least have known that they were dealing with an honestly growling wolf, rather than a fox who could have them half-digested before they even knew what was happening." Negroes, of course, had voted overwhelmingly for Johnson, who was promoting civil rights legislation.

By that time, Malcolm had broken with Elijah Muhammad and had rejected the simplistic teaching that all whites were devils, but he was totally devoted to black nationalism:

Why black nationalism? Well, in the competitive American society, how can there ever be any white-black solidarity before there is first some black solidarity? If you will remember, in my childhood I had been exposed to the black nationalist teachings of Marcus Garvey—which, in fact, I had been told had led to my father's murder. Even when I was a follower of Elijah Muhammad, I had been strongly aware of how the black nationalist political, economic and social philosophies had the ability to instill within black men the racial dignity, the incentive, and the confidence that the black race needs today to get up off its knees, and to get on its feet, and get rid of its scars, and to take a stand for itself. . . . I said to Harlem street audiences . . . that on the American racial level, we had to approach the black man's struggle against the white

man's racism as a human problem, that we had to forget hypocriti-
cal politics and propaganda. I said that both races, as human
beings, had the obligation, the responsibility, of helping to correct
America's human problem. The well-meaning white people, I said,
had to combat actively and directly, the racism of other white
people. And the black people had to build within themselves much
greater awareness that along with equal rights there had to be the
bearing of equal responsibilities.

This philosophy within a few years would become widely
accepted among black leaders in the Northern cities and
among many who participated in the integration movement
in the South.

Even so, black nationalism was very much a minority
movement among Negroes prior to 1966. In 1964, Dr. King
wrote that the new militancy shown by participants in the
nonviolent movement had prevented the appeal of the
separatists from becoming general. "As I travel throughout
the country," he said, "I am struck by how few American
Negroes, except in a handful of big-city ghettos, have even
heard of the Muslim movement, much less given allegiance
to its pessimistic doctrine." The public opinion polls at the
time bore him out. But forces that were then at work would
within the decade change the picture considerably in behalf
of nationalism, North and South.

For some time there had been nascent nationalism among
Negro leaders who had been promoting integration, some
who were closely associated with Dr. King. The nonviolent
movement had been built to some extent on the white liberal
movement in behalf of Negro equality that grew out of the
New Deal and its many ramifications. One of the roots of this
movement was the Myrdal study, *An American Dilemma*,

which constituted a thorough documentation and analysis of the racial problem at the beginning of World War II. So thoroughly had racism been engrained in the society, Myrdal wrote later, that he was "shocked and scared to the bones by all the evils I saw and by the serious political implications of the problem." But he found hope for change in the fact that so many Americans subscribed to the national creed of liberty and justice for all. The "old Americans," Myrdal wrote, those who came early and have prospered, adhere to the creed as the faith of their ancestors while the disadvantaged —the Negroes and other minority groups—could not have invented a system of political ideals that would serve them better. "So, by the logic of the unique American history, it has developed that the rich and secure, out of pride and conservatism, and the poor and insecure, out of dire need, have come to profess the identical social ideals."

The key to the problem, then, Myrdal concluded, "is in the heart of the American. It is there that the interracial tension has its focus. It is there that the decisive struggle goes on." By exploiting the conflict between what white Americans believe and what they do in regard to Negroes, Myrdal said, black people eventually would find the justice and equality of treatment that they sought. "America's handling of the Negro problem has been criticized most emphatically by white Americans since long before the Revolution," Myrdal noted, "and the criticism has steadily gone on and will not stop until America has completely reformed itself."

To a large extent, the nonviolent movement was directed to the dilemma in the heart of white America. But after a time both blacks and whites in the movement began to have doubts about the troubled heart of white America. In 1964, Charles E. Silberman wrote in *Crisis in Black and White*:

What we are discovering, in short, is that the United States—all of it, North as well as South, West as well as East—is a racist society in a sense and to a degree that we have refused so far to admit, much less face. . . . Myrdal was wrong. The tragedy of race relations in the United States is that there is no American Dilemma. White Americans are not torn and tortured by the conflict between their devotion to the American creed and their actual behavior. They are upset by the current state of race relations, to be sure. But what troubles them is not that justice is being denied but that their peace is being shattered and their business interrupted.

This, of course, was what the black nationalists had been saying all along. There were in the nonviolent movement throughout the nation young leaders who were beginning to give up on white America and wonder whether a separate society of some kind might not be more promising than integration into white institutions. There were many reasons why this was so. They can be explained partly through the experiences of the Student Nonviolent Coordinating Committee, which during the mid-1960's underwent a radical transformation. SNCC was organized by Dr. King and others to give youths, who were becoming increasingly restless and anxious to participate in the freedom movement, an outlet for participation in all kinds of protest. It was at first thoroughly nonviolent and drew its membership from both blacks and whites. Its field workers were dedicated young people who worked for a meager allowance and lived among the poor they were trying to help.

In the early 1960's, SNCC became a cutting edge of the nonviolent movement. Not only did it supply many of the participants for the big-city crusades that King and others led, but it also went first into the rural areas of the deep South, where the resistance was strongest, the organizing the most difficult, and the physical danger the greatest. John Lewis, who was then chairman of SNCC, held the record, as far as anyone knew, for having been beaten and jailed more than anyone else in the movement. Men such as James Forman, Stokely Carmichael, Ivanhoe Donaldson, and Bob Moses were accustomed to having their heads knocked, without benefit of ceremony or publicity, before country court houses and on dusty back roads while Dr. King and other leaders were appearing on national television. The wonder was that they did not lose faith in white America sooner than they did.

SNCC's big undertaking was the Mississippi Summer Project of 1964. It was organized by Bob Moses, a quiet young math teacher who had come South from Harlem and opened up several rural areas to the civil rights movement. The project was ambitious, idealistic, and was set up with all of the nonviolent movement's faith in a shared society. Moses went to college campuses across the country and recruited students, black and white, to spend the summer in Mississippi helping the blacks there to gain their freedom. They came by the hundreds, constituting what James W. Silver, the historian, called "a super Peace Corps willing to move constantly in the shadow of violence and death for nothing more or less than the implementation of the promise of democracy and equality in the Declaration of Independence." They taught in freedom schools, conducted voter registration drives, built community centers, set up health clinics, established black cooperatives, provided legal assistance, staffed day-care centers, and conducted free theater.

During the summer, the youths and Mississippi Negroes suffered several violent deaths—including those of Michael Schwerner, Andrew Goodman, and James Chaney, the three youths who were abducted, shot, and buried under a dam on the day the project opened—scores of injuries and hundreds of arrests. From many aspects, the project was a success. It had attracted national attention, given SNCC new support and prestige nationally, and opened Mississippi for further civil rights advances.

But the SNCC leaders were less than enthralled with the results. The project had attracted persons from a wide range of ideologies. Some who came were of the New Left and some of their literature and teachings got into the freedom schools. This upset many of the local Negro leaders who believed the Negro protest should be made, for practical reasons, only within the framework of traditional American democracy. So there was division within the Negro leadership that appeared ominous to SNCC.

There was a feeling among many black leaders, too, that whites had played too large a role in the project. Although the project was largely the work of Bob Moses, who was black, whites had moved in and virtually taken over in a number of areas. There was the story of the bright white girl from Mt. Holyoke who brought her electric typewriter and replaced several Negro girls who were learning to peck on ancient machines. There was a new awareness throughout the movement of the need for blacks to find their own identity and manage their own affairs, and the presence of white organization and management was considered by some black leaders to be a new form of "colonialism."

Then there was the matter of politics. SNCC had organized the Mississippi Freedom Democratic Party in an effort to extend the ballot to blacks, who had been barred from the polls for generations. The Freedom Party conducted mock elections to train Negroes in the voting processes and to demonstrate how a large segment of the population had been denied political representation. At the Democratic National Convention in Atlantic City, the Freedom Party challenged the Mississippi regulars for the state's seats, charging the regulars with unlawfully holding their position by preventing blacks from participating in the established party. The national Democrats tried to strike a compromise that would later lead to integration of the Mississippi party. As offered by the credentials committee and approved by the White House, the compromise would have required that the regulars take the loyalty oath in support of the national platform and candidates, that two delegates from the Freedom Democrats be seated with the regulars, and steps be taken to assure that thereafter the state party processes would be open to all eligible regardless of race. The national party was attempting to achieve a traditional political solution that would retain both black and white support for the Democrats in Mississippi. But Bob Moses and other SNCC leaders considered it an outrage. They believed they had proved the regular state party to be racist and corrupt, yet it was permitted to retain most of the power it had. The Freedom Party delegates returned to Mississippi deeply embittered. "The major moral of that experience," Stokely Carmichael and Charles V. Hamilton wrote three years later in *Black Power, the Politics of Liberation in America*, "was not merely that the national conscience was generally unreliable but that, very specifically, black people in Mississippi and throughout this country could not rely on their so-called allies."

There were similar disillusioning incidents in other states and in the summer and fall of 1965 developments within the national government caused further dismay among black leaders. At mid-summer, President Johnson announced the first large commitment of resources and manpower to the war in Vietnam. Although on June 4 he had delivered a stirring address at Howard University calling for a renewed national effort to help blacks secure those rights promised them by law, it was soon apparent as the summer wore on that the President had set a higher priority—winning the struggle in Southeast Asia. The President's attention, the best talent in the government, and billions of dollars that Negro leaders had hoped would go into social programs were turned to Vietnam. It was apparent, too, that the so-called war on poverty, begun with great promise a few months previously, was more on the order of a skirmish and was not of sufficient scale to make significant change.

Negro leaders were alarmed, too, that the Johnson Administration was being very cautious in its enforcement of the new civil rights laws. For example, the 1964 Act contained a provision banning racial discrimination in any federally assisted program. Because of its vast system of subsidies touching almost every area of public life, the federal government now had the authority to move immediately and massively against segregation in schools, hospitals, agricultural services, and many other institutions. Yet the bureaucracy was slow to move and by fall virtually all of the national Negro leaders, moderates as well as militants, were complaining of broken promises and failure of enforcement.

At the same time, violence broke out in many urban slums. One of the ironies of the period was the fact that in the days that the Justice Department began to enforce the Voting Rights Act, which promised political power to scores of thousands of Negroes in the South, the Watts section of Los Angeles was erupting in rioting, burning, and looting. The same phenomenon was seen on a lesser scale in a number of other cities. This had an important impact on the nation and on the thinking of Negro leaders who had participated in the nonviolent movement. Even the moderate civil rights leaders agreed that for all that had been done in the South, poor blacks in the slums had scarcely been touched by the movement. Stokely Carmichael, by then chairman of SNCC, said in September of the following year:

One of the tragedies of the struggle against racism is that up to now there had been no national organization which could speak to the growing militancy of young black people in the urban ghetto. There has been only a civil rights movement, whose tone of voice was adapted to an audience of liberal whites. It served as a sort of buffer zone between them and angry young blacks. None of its so-called leaders could go into a rioting community and be listened to. . . . For too many years, black Americans marched and had their heads broken and got shot. They were saying to the country, "Look, you guys are supposed to be nice guys and we are only going to do what we are supposed to do—why do you beat us up, why don't you give us what we ask, why don't you straighten yourselves out?" After years of this, we are at almost the same point—because we demonstrated from a position of weakness. We cannot be expected any longer to march and have our heads broken in order to say to whites: come on, you're nice guys. For you are not nice guys. We have found you out.

By the summer of 1966, Carmichael and other young black leaders who had been active in the nonviolent movement began to chant "Black Power" on marches through the South, and the meaning of the slogan was defined in a "position paper" worked out by the SNCC leadership. It called for withdrawal of whites from the organization and for Negroes to develop a nationalistic view of themselves—as "exploited colonials." Negroes should develop their own businesses, cooperatives, and power bases. The technique of nonviolence was dropped by the organization and the leaders advised blacks to fight back when attacked. The Congress of Racial Equality, which had its roots in the pacifist movement, moved in the same direction, and its nonviolent leaders, James Farmer and others, were forced out.

After the summer of 1965, a rapid polarization took place, both between blacks and whites and within the black leadership. The old-line organizations such as the NAACP and the Urban League stuck to nonviolence and integration while CORE and SNCC were moving to violence and separatism. King and his Southern Christian Leadership Conference tried to steer a middle course, but his influence was clearly on the decline, as was the entire civil rights movement. The White House seemed to increase the breach by honoring and praising the moderates and rejecting the militants. The urban riots, which grew worse each year until 1968, increased white hostilities, which brought more distrust among blacks. And in 1968 the National Advisory Commission on Civil Disorders (the Kerner Commission) found that "our nation is moving toward two societies, one black, one white—separate and unequal."

Moderate Negro leaders have complained that the news media gave too much attention to leaders such as Carmichael and his successor, Rap Brown, who by 1967 was traveling the country saying, "If America don't come around, we going to burn it down, brother. We are going to burn it down if we don't get our share of it." It is true that the changes among the Negro leadership had little effect on the goals of the masses of Negroes, most of whom went right on favoring integration, according to the opinion polls and other studies.

The emerging nationalists were important, nevertheless, for the effect they had on the movement and in the fact that in one sense they were not so much leading as responding to the desires of substantial numbers of activists who began to find the teachings of Malcolm X more and more appealing. It was not long after 1965 that most of the educated young blacks in the cities, the opinion-makers of the future, were saying that separatism was desirable, at least for a time.

4

Confusion in a Dream Deferred

We wear the mask that grins and lies,
It hides our cheeks and shades our eyes,
> —PAUL LAURENCE DUNBAR
> (1872–1906)

. . . it's all jungle here, a wild and savage
wilderness that's overrun with ruins.
> **ELDRIDGE CLEAVER**
> *Soul on Ice,* 1968

There's liable
to be confusion
in a dream deferred.
> —LANGSTON HUGHES
> (1902–1967)

We are waiting for a new God.
> —JEAN TOOMER
> (1894–1967)

THE VOICES of black poets and writers speak eloquently of a difficulty that Negroes have faced ever since their arrival in this country, a difficulty that today remains central to the question of Negro goals—the problem of identity in a society that was built for and is run largely by whites. It is common to hear a person of Irish, Italian, or Jewish descent say, "We knew the worst kind of discrimination. We were poor and

47

despised and lived in the slums. But by hard work and sacrifice we pulled ourselves out of it. Why can't they?"

The fact that in 1972, after all that has occurred in recent years, whites still make such statements causes some blacks to agree with Eldridge Cleaver that "it's all jungle here." For no other group in this country—not the Jews, the European ethnics, the Appalachian whites, the Mexican Americans, the Asians, not even the American Indians—has had an experience that has any resemblance to that of Negro Americans.

They were brought here in slavery, severed from their African past, their language, their very names, and required to live under a society that placed a high premium on family and morality and on male leadership but then made it so that blacks could acquire these traits only under the most difficult and rare circumstances. Even after winning a semblance of liberty and civil rights, the life of every Negro was framed by the white society into which he could never enter freely but that shaped his own thoughts about himself.

Ralph Ellison, in the prologue to his famous novel, *Invisible Man*, stated one of the effects:

I am an invisible man. . . . I am invisible, understand, simply because people refuse to see me. Like the bodiless heads you see sometimes in circus sideshows, it is as though I have been surrounded by mirrors of hard distorting glass. When they approach me they see only my surroundings, themselves, or figments of their imagination—indeed, everything and anything except me. . . . You wonder whether you aren't simply a phantom in other people's minds. Say, a figure in a nightmare which the sleeper tries with all his strength to destroy. It's when you feel like this that, out of resentment, you begin to bump people back. And, let me confess, you feel that way most of the time. You ache with the need to convince yourself that you do exist in the real world, that you're a part of all the sound and anguish, and you strike out with your fists, you curse and you swear to make them recognize you. And, alas, it's seldom successful.

Worse yet was the extent to which many Negroes accepted the white society's belief that whites were superior and Negroes inferior. Stokely Carmichael, after his conversion to "Black Power," recalled how Negroes from birth were told, and believed, lies about themselves. "I remember when I was a boy," he said, "I used to go to Tarzan movies on Saturday. White Tarzan used to beat up the black natives. I would sit there yelling, 'Kill the beasts, kill the savages, kill 'em!' I was saying: Kill *me*. It was as if a Jewish boy watched Nazis taking Jews off to concentration camps and cheered them on. Today, I want the chief to beat hell out of Tarzan and send him back to Europe."

Once Negroes subscribed to the belief in white superiority they found themselves in a tortured position of trying to emulate the characteristics of whites. Malcolm X, in his autobiography, told of receiving as a young man in Boston his first "conk," or hair straightening, from a pale yellowish mixture of lye, potatoes, and raw eggs. After a long period of applying the mixture and rinsing it out, his hair hung down in limp, damp strings:

My scalp still flamed, but not as badly: I could bear it. He [a friend named Shorty] draped the towel around my shoulders, over my rubber apron, and began again vaselining my hair.

I could feel him combing, straight back, first the big comb, then the fine-tooth one. . . . My first view in the mirror blotted out the hurting. I'd seen some pretty conks, but when it's the first time, on your *own* head, the transformation, after the lifetime of kinks, is staggering.

The mirror reflected Shorty behind me. We both were grinning and sweating. And on top of my head was this thick, smooth sheen of shining red hair—real red—as straight as any white man's.

How ridiculous I was! Stupid enough to stand there simply lost in admiration of my hair now looking "white," reflected in the mirror in Shorty's room. I vowed that I'd never again be without a conk, and I never was for many years.

The extent of the identity problem is suggested by the acceptability or unacceptability of the words "Negro," "black," "Afro-American," and so on. A recent cartoon in *The New Yorker* magazine showed a white woman at a cocktail party asking a black couple, "What are you people calling yourselves these days?" A middle-aged Negro leader in Oakland, California, was asked somewhat the same thing by a white reporter. He replied, "If they are under thirty, you can feel sure that they would want to be called black and might feel offended if you referred to them constantly as Negroes. With older people, you can feel safe in calling them Negroes because they can remember the day when black was a derisive term and some of them worked all their lives trying to get white people to pronounce Negro properly. People of my age probably would accept either term, though I myself still find black a little offensive. Afro-American, well it's just sort of a neutral term but hasn't caught on much."

In this book, the words Negro and black are used interchangeably in view of the wide acceptance of both terms. A few years ago, however, a writer sensitive to race relations would not have used black. Its acceptability among Negroes grew out of the black nationalist movement, which rejected the term Negro. The word in itself had no bad connotation, but the black nationalists, who were trying to get away from all-white influences, rejected it because it was considered a white-man's term. The rapid ascendancy of the use of the term black was one indication of a rather wide acceptance of some degree of black nationalism. By 1967, the slogan "black is beautiful" was popular in most segments of the Negro movement.

Although it certainly is nothing new, the emergence of black pride is considered among blacks of various persuasions to be one of the most liberating influences of the recent Negro movement. Countless blacks across the nation are growing up without the hang-ups that Ralph Ellison, Richard Wright, James Baldwin, and many others wrote about. Charles Browser, a bright black leader in Philadelphia, said in an interview early in 1970: "My wife is not teaching our kids what my mother taught me, to stay in your place. My young son might get killed in this country but he knows he's free. I took him to Washington with me the other day and he spoke right up to the taxi driver and said, 'Hey, are there many black people here?' He's proud to be black."

The black consciousness movement is important to the subject of Negro goals because it was brought to the forefront by the black nationalists who contended that pride in their race could not be engendered as long as white people were around running things. This contention is open to dispute. The nonviolent movement had a strong element of black pride. Dr. King repeatedly emphasized this, calling it "somebodiness." One wonders if the self-disciplined blacks who marched in St. Augustine, Albany, and Birmingham in the face of white oppression did not have a more viable kind of black pride than those who followed Rap Brown's advice and burned the cities. The Reverend Andrew Young, one of Dr. King's chief aides, said in an interview in 1969, "We never had the problems that SNCC and other groups did about whites taking over, so we did not have the kind of reaction to it that they did. In our organization [the Southern Christian Leadership Conference] whites participated but they were always in a subservient role, and that's the way it has to be."

Nor was it true that nonviolence reached only the middle class. In St. Augustine, for example, almost the entire community of poor blacks was led into the most disciplined kind of nonviolent protest. But it was true that Carmichael, Malcolm X, and others could with their brand of black consciousness "turn on" countless Negroes who previously had not been reached. Black consciousness seemed to have more appeal when Carmichael said, "Integration today means the man who 'makes it,' leaving his black brothers behind in the ghetto as fast as his sports car will take him. . . . Integration, moreover, speaks to the problem of blackness in a despicable way. As a goal, it has been based on the complete acceptance of the fact that in order to have a decent house or education, blacks must move into a white neighborhood or send their children to a white school. This reinforces, among both black and white, the idea that 'white' is automatically better and 'black' is by definition inferior. This is why integration is a subterfuge for the maintenance of white supremacy."

The racial struggles of the 1950's and 1960's, in which the leaders and intellectuals were moving rapidly from one position to another, left a wide variety of opinions among the nation's 22 million blacks as to what they sought in the American society. Whites tend to overemphasize the solidarity of the Negro community, because they are a people with a common problem. But the black population of this country has never been solid of opinion, any more than the South, the Roman Catholic Church, or the Congress of the United States. The goals of blacks are many and it is not unusual for people to honor Malcolm X and Marcus Garvey without subscribing at all to their teachings. And there is ambiguity within individuals. In a little book entitled *Black Is*, Turner Brown, Jr., wrote that black is, among other things, "getting kicks from Rap and Stokely but hoping Martin Luther King was right." And the two chief heroes of young blacks in colleges today are, side by side, Malcolm X and Martin Luther King.

Black leaders have acknowledged that there is a "level of rhetoric and a level of reality" in the Negro community, a posture that has evolved over the years out of the efforts of Negroes to "get the man off our back." Much of the black power phenomenon fell into this category. Robert W. Friedrichs, writing in the *Yale Review* in the spring of 1968, said that the outpouring of black anger was, in effect, "cries of pain" from people who previously were forced to turn their aggressions inward:

The phenomenon of black power, then, comes to be seen for what it functionally is: not primarily an effective political movement *per se* (though political activity looking for grass-roots support among Negroes at the present moment would have to ride its crest rather than deny it) but rather a necessary stage on the long trek back to psychic and social health—health systematically denied the black man in America for some three hundred years. The same is true of other manifestations of verbal violence burgeoning over the last few years, starting perhaps with the hints dropped by Genet's perversely perceptive *The Blacks*, breaking out of the black underworld and a narrow Muslim cultism through the charismatic tutelage of Malcolm X, parlayed in the arts for the edification of the black bourgeoisie by Leroi Jones, consciously appropriated by such middle-class youths as Stokely Carmichael and H. Rap Brown who, though personally temperate, saw it for the portentous weapon for mass psychic liberation it was.

This would explain, perhaps, why the goals of the black nationalists have never been fully defined. Malcolm X was in the process of developing his when he was killed. SNCC, on adopting black power and forsaking nonviolence, fast disintegrated into a shadow organization, changing its name along the way to the Student National Coordinating Committee, and was succeeded by the Black Panther Party, which advocates overthrow of the system and institution of a socialist state. The Congress of Racial Equality advocated a separate black economy, with certain reservations, but declined greatly from the large national organization that it was under the nonviolent movement.

Only the old-line organizations such as the NAACP and the Urban League, and to some extent the Southern Christian Leadership Conference, which kept touch with all factions, remained large and effective national organizations, and they stood, as they always had, for protest and integration, even though they made some accommodations for young militants who were leaning to separatism. Carmichael, Roy Innis of CORE, James Forman, Malcolm X, and others all wanted to provide national leadership and a viable program for the lower-class blacks in the cities who would never follow nonviolence, but none of their movements could be sustained. In a sense, their movements suffered the same fate as had those started by Bishop Turner and Marcus Garvey. Built on a negative base of alienation and distrust of whites, they splintered or evaporated. Only the Panthers and Muslims remained as national organizations; their influence and membership were very limited. And the majority of nationalists apparently considered neither movement to be viable.

What remained in the black nationalist movement was

Balkanized local and regional organizations with various goals. The Muslims were still acquiring property and land, their total membership remaining at about 100,000. Several small and seemingly transitory groups in New York, Detroit, Chicago, and other cities set out to acquire, somehow, separate states. The Black Economic Development Conference, which attracted Forman after he experienced an unhappy sojourn with the Panthers, carried its "Black Manifesto" to the white churches, demanding $3 billion in reparations for past injustices to blacks, but there was no indication that the conference had widespread support among the black population.

Against this background we can now look with more precision and understanding at what blacks are demanding and expecting from America.

5

Black Attitudes

IN A BLACK neighborhood of San Francisco one day in 1969, a mother of twelve sat in her upstairs tenement apartment and described for a visitor her difficulties of the previous few years finding a place for her family to live. The building she was in was scheduled for demolition under urban renewal and she was demanding that the authorities find a similar location at least as "good." Would it not be better for the children, she was asked, if she could locate a house or apartment in an outlying area where there would be more room for play and less exposure to crime, delinquency, and narcotics?

"Move to the suburbs?" she exploded. "Well, let me tell *you,* a few years ago I wanted to move to a nice quiet suburban neighborhood, anywhere I could find, but they soon let me know I wasn't wanted in the suburbs. Oh, how I wanted to go. Maybe with the fair housing laws that had been passed since I could now find a place somewhere. But I have decided I don't *want* to move to the suburbs where I am not wanted. I want to stay here in *this* neighborhood where there are other poor blacks and where we are organizing for community action."

In one sense, the San Francisco mother could be described as a separatist, but her separatism was shaped by the attitudes of the white majority around her. And the visitor got the clear impression that if white attitudes moderated somewhat her newly acquired inclination to black solidarity would evaporate overnight.

When the black power movement with its accent on separatism sprang into prominence in the mid-1960's, the people who measure public opinion began taking polls of America's Negro population to see whether the movement gained public favor. A number of such polls were taken, nationally and locally, between 1964 and 1970, and they showed rather conclusively that the great majority of Negroes do not advocate separatism. Despite great changes in the Negro leadership, the goals as expressed by the great mass of Negroes has remained rather constant. But the findings are not without paradox and there could be a great danger in oversimplification.

Probably the most comprehensive survey was one conducted for the National Advisory Commission on Civil Disorders early in 1968 and published in July of that year, several months after the commission's main report had been issued. The survey was conducted under a Ford Foundation grant and headed by Angus Campbell and Howard Schuman of the University of Michigan. Both white and Negro attitudes were measured in 5,759 interviews conducted in fifteen cities—Baltimore, Boston, Chicago, Cincinnati, Cleveland, Detroit, Gary, Milwaukee, Newark, New York, Philadelphia, Pittsburgh, San Francisco, St. Louis, and Washington, D. C. Negroes questioned constituted a scientific sample of 3,330,000, ages sixteen to sixty-nine living in the fifteen cities, all of which had undergone civil disorders of some magnitude. If there were separatism and black militancy among Negroes in the United States it was to be found there.

Almost half of the Negro sample indicated a preference for living in a mixed neighborhood and another third said that the racial character of the neighborhood made no difference to them. Here is the breakdown of the response to the question, "Would you personally prefer to live in a neighborhood with all Negroes, mostly Negroes, mostly whites, or a neighborhood that is mixed half and half?"

	(IN PERCENT)		
	MEN	WOMEN	TOTAL
All Negro	7	8	8
Mostly Negro	7	4	5
Mostly white	1	1	1
Mixed half and half	47	48	48
Makes no difference	37	37	37
Don't know	1	2	1
	100	100	100

A better idea of the extent of separatist thinking can be seen in the following table, which shows the percentages responding affirmatively to specific kinds of separatism.

	MEN	WOMEN	TOTAL
Believe stores in a "Negro neighborhood" should be owned and run by Negroes	21	15	18
Believe school with mostly Negro children should have Negro principal	17	12	14
Believe school with mostly Negro children should have mostly Negro teachers	13	7	10
Agree that "Negroes should have nothing to do with whites if they can help it"	11	8	9
Believe whites should be discouraged from taking part in civil rights organizations	9	6	8
Believe close friendship between Negroes and whites is impossible	6	5	6

Agree that "there should be separate black nation here"	7	4	6
Prefer child to have only Negro friends, not white friends too	6	4	5

"Both in their personal lives and on issues concerning public institutions, Negroes in these fifteen cities oppose black separatism by an overwhelming margin," the authors of the survey wrote. "The largest support for racial exclusiveness turns on the ownership by Negroes of stores in a Negro neighborhood, which is supported by nearly one out of five members of the sample; yet even on this highly publicized current issue, four out of five respondents refuse to introduce race as a criterion for ownership or control."

Still, this did not answer *why* the Negroes interviewed gave the answers they did. The authors pointed out that it could be argued that the responses were for pragmatic reasons—that is, they perceived that services in white or mixed neighborhoods tended to be better than in all black neighborhoods. The survey found this to be true to some extent. For example, 24 percent of those questioned said they preferred mixed schools because they considered the facilities and teaching better. But 30 percent said they believed that black and white children should learn to get along with one another and another 30 percent said they simply believed race should not make any difference.

"It is clear," the authors said, "that in early 1968 the major commitment of the great majority of the Negro population in these fifteen cities was not to racial exclusiveness insofar as this meant personal rejection of whites or an emphasis on racial considerations in running community institutions. Negroes hold strongly, perhaps more strongly than

59

any other element in the American population, to a belief in nondiscrimination and racial harmony."

Another aspect of the survey dealt with Negro leadership. At the time it was taken, it should be remembered, the nonviolent movement was in decline, Martin Luther King was discouraged about the amount of racial bitterness shown by both blacks and whites, the black power movement had had time to mature, and the urban riots were at their peak. Those interviewed were asked this question: "Now I want to read you a list of people active in civil rights. For each one, please tell me whether you approve or disapprove of what the person stands for, or don't know enough about him to say." The following tables show a part of the results, in percentages.

	MEN	WOMEN	TOTAL
Martin Luther King			
Approve	70	74	72
Partly approve, partly disapprove	22	16	19
Disapprove	5	4	5
Don't know	3	6	4
Roy Wilkins (NAACP head)			
Approve	54	46	50
Partly approve, partly disapprove	13	11	12
Disapprove	4	2	3
Don't know	29	41	35
Stokely Carmichael			
Approve	18	10	14
Partly approve, partly disapprove	24	17	21
Disapprove	34	36	35
Don't know	24	37	50
How About the NAACP?			
Approve	77	74	75
Partly approve, partly disapprove	12	10	11
Disapprove	3	3	3
Don't know	8	13	11

It can be seen, then, that Dr. King and his advocacy of nonviolence, coupled with strong protests over the discrimination against blacks, still had strong support among

Negroes, while Stokely Carmichael, if he was known at all, had minority support. And the NAACP, the old-line rights organization that had consistently stood for integration, was very much in favor. And the authors noted that the approval acknowledged for leaders such as Carmichael was not so much for their advocacy of specific programs and goals as for "their emphasis on the serious difficulties Negroes face and the vociferous attribution of those difficulties to white America."

One of the early studies of Negro attitudes in the 1960's was made by the University of California's Survey Research Center for the Anti-Defamation League of B'nai B'rith. The findings, based on interviews taken late in 1964, were published in 1967 in a book entitled *Protest and Prejudice* by Gary T. Marx. Despite the great changes that took place in the Negro movement after those interviews, a new edition of the book was brought out in 1969 with the full confidence of the author that it was still current. In a postscript, Marx said that fifteen subsequent studies or polls showed that the "mass moderation" he had found among Negroes was little changed. All of the findings were along the lines of those reported by the Kerner Commission.

"Between 1964 and 1968 the relative power of the more militant groups seems to have greatly increased," Marx wrote, "yet the data [studies and surveys] suggests that there has not been a comparable increase in mass support."

Marx pointed out that to Negroes the term black power, which had frightened great numbers of whites, was not synonymous with violence, racism, or black rule over whites and was in keeping with American pluralism that had worked to the benefit of other minorities. Black power, said a young Detroit militant, "means mostly equality. You know, to have power to go up to a person, you know, no matter what his skin color and be accepted on the same level, you know, and it doesn't necessarily have to mean that you gotta take over everything and be a revolutionary and all this: just as long as people are going to respect you, you know, for what you are as a person and not, you know, what your skin color has to do with the thing."

The question remaining was how much power and influence the separatists have now and will have in the future. Moderate Negro leaders have said repeatedly that the separatist leaders have virtually no following; that is, they have not influenced many to accept their goals. Nevertheless, as the study for the Kerner Commission pointed out, "small percentages can represent large numbers." Campbell and Schuman pointed out that in the fifteen cities they studied one percent of the Negro sample stands for about 33,000 people:

Thus, when we say that six percent of the sample advocates the formation of a separate black nation, we are implying that some 200,000 Negroes in these 15 cities feel so little a part of American society that they favor withdrawing allegiance from the United States and in some sense establishing a separate national entity. Unlike election polls where it is usually correct to focus on majority or at least plurality figures, "small" percentages in this study must not be disregarded as unimportant. In a formal election six percent of the vote means little, but in a campaign to change minds and influence policies, six percent of a population can represent a considerable force. This is particularly true when the six percent represents deviation from a traditional position, since it is likely that many of those who hold to the majority position do so with little thought or commitment. To deviate from a widely held norm probably requires more conviction than to hold to it, and if we could estimate this extra factor and weight it into the results we might well find the force behind black nationalism to be considerably greater than its numbers suggest.

Another factor in this regard is that separatism seems to be more popular among the young—those who will be in a position to influence public opinion in the future—than among the elderly and middle-aged. This is shown in the following table from the Kerner Commission study:

Separatist Thinking by Age
[in percentages]

	Negro Men					
Ages	16-19	20-29	30-39	40-49	50-59	60-69
Believe stores in Negro neighborhoods should be owned, run by Negroes	28	23	20	18	14	18
Believe school with mostly Negro children should have mostly Negro teachers	22	15	13	6	5	15
Agree that Negroes should have nothing to do with whites if they can help it	18	14	6	12	4	13
Believe whites should be discouraged from taking part in rights organizations	19	12	8	6	3	5
Agree that there should be a separate black nation here	11	10	5	5	4	10
	Negro Women					
Believe stores in Negro neighborhoods should be owned, run by Negroes	18	16	16	15	13	8
Believe school with mostly Negro children should have mostly Negro teachers	11	9	6	5	5	12
Agree that Negroes should have nothing to do with whites if they can help it	11	7	7	8	5	7
Believe whites should be discouraged from taking part in civil rights organizations	11	7	7	5	7	3
Agree that there should be a separate black nation here	9	3	2	6	4	3

The table shows that in general younger Negroes assert separatist beliefs more strongly than do older Negroes. There is a "doubling back" of the older males that the authors of the survey said probably amounted to "irrelevant artifact." My own suspicion, without having facts to base it on, is that the older group better remembers the atrocious treatment of Negroes early in the century and was of impressionable age when the Garvey movement and other nationalist trends were on the rise after World War I. The younger groups came of age when Negroes at last were beginning to make some progress toward equality and there were some signs of hope for blacks within white America. The authors pointed out that if the older group is ignored, "the changes between the 50 to 59 and the 16 to 19 represents at least a doubling of percent separatist thinking for women and a tripling for men."

Young blacks coming of age in the 1960's were able to see with clarity, perhaps for the first time, what white society had done to their people, psychologically as well as materially. Not only had Negroes been excluded and made a people of inferior position, but whites had then defined the condition and causes of black inferiority so that the burden of responsibility lay not on the oppressor but the oppressed. And to make matters worse, Negroes by the millions had accepted the white man's definitions because whites so thoroughly controlled the society under which Negroes lived. Young blacks, when they saw this, were understandably angry and ready to accept the idea that the only hope for blacks was to set *themselves* apart, make their own definitions, and free the minds of their own people before they could consider living in the white society.

Campbell and Schuman said there was a hint in their findings that institutional self-rule appealed to more educated Negroes, while wholesale rejection of whites appealed to the less educated. This would conform to the patterns of the past. It will be remembered that the Turner and Garvey movements appealed largely to the black lower class while the blacks of more education in those days were trying to find more sophisticated ways toward black salvation. In any event the development of black pride and self-determination has wide appeal within the urban Negro population, and this does not necessarily mean any more separatism than has been practiced by American ethnic groups that have been mostly assimilated into the larger society. The following table from the Kerner Commission study shows the extent of positive cultural identity:

Percentages of Negroes Expressing Approval

	MEN	WOMEN	TOTAL
Negroes should take more pride in Negro history	96	96	96
There should be more Negro business, banks and stores	95	92	94
Negros should shop in Negro owned stores whenever possible	70	69	70
Negro school children should study an African language	46	38	42

"As in the case of religious and ethnic groups in America," the authors of the report concluded, "there seems to be wide support for cultural individuality *within* a larger interracial social structure. Such affirmation of black identity is in keeping with American pluralism and should not be termed 'separatism.' It does, however, contain a source from which leaders advocating separatism can draw, especially if there is wide disillusionment with the possibility of making integration work in social and political contexts."

This trend toward "American pluralism" has been seen in numbers of ways. For example, thousands of Negroes subscribed to stock in a new bank which opened in 1970 in downtown Detroit amid white-owned businesses, so that blacks who worked downtown could use the bank and thus accumulate capital to use to start black-owned businesses in black neighborhoods. The young president, David Harper, was asked by a reporter before the bank opened what all this meant. "It simply means we are acting like the Italians, the Germans and the Poles have in this country for years. Money is what is important. You can't have power without it. So we are carrying out an honored American tradition, that is all." This was, indeed, a far cry from the separatism taught by Bishop Turner, Garvey, and the Black Muslims. For the Negroes working downtown already were integrated into the American business world and the bank was only a means of giving Negroes, as a group, more power, wealth and influence in the overall society.

The authors of the Kerner Commission survey said in conclusion that "while there is no doubt that Negroes want change and some of them are prepared to do desperate things to bring it about, the changes they have in mind are essentially conservative in nature. The great majority do not propose to withdraw from America; they want equal status in it. They do not talk of tearing down the economic and political institutions of the nation; they seek to share equally in the benefits. The majority—but in this case no longer the *great* majority—are not despondent and without hope for the future; they see 'real progress' over the last decade and real hope for the future."

The qualification that the authors made to this is important, too:

There is a large minority—a full third of the urban sample—that does *not* believe "real progress" has been made for most Negroes over the decade and a half since the 1954 Supreme Court school desegregation decision. There is an even larger proportion who believe discrimination in employment and housing are major facts of life for Negroes today—facts of life that are not getting much better. Whether they are correct or incorrect in their belief, these discontented people make up a third of our sample and, in numerical terms, more than a million teenage and adult Negroes in these 15 major cities. Largely contained within this third is a much smaller group of individuals who see violence as necessary to right injustices they believe are the lot of the Negro in America. This group is small but not trivial in numbers. More important, these individuals have the sympathy and perhaps to some extent the support of the larger minority discussed above. The most important fact about those inclined toward violence is that they are not an isolated band of deviants condemned by almost all other Negroes, but are linked to a much larger group by a common definition of the problems that beset the Negro in America.

Subsequent events and studies substantiated this conclusion. When the police in Chicago raided a building occupied by Black Panthers, resulting in several deaths, moderate Negroes who had no use for the revolutionary goals espoused by the Panthers rose in their defense. Almost every city across the country has at least one militant black leader who preaches overturn of the present government, and while the moderates do not share this view they defend his right to be a leader of black people and in fact believe that he has a constructive role in the struggle for Negro equality. It is the revolutionaries, they say, who remind white leaders of the dangers inherent in continued discrimination against Negroes.

6

Community Control

NO DISCUSSION of black goals would be complete without going to some extent into the meaning of community control, one of the catch words of the Negro movement that came into vogue following the decline of nonviolence. The ambiguity of this term can be pointed up by the fact that while many whites considered it radical and one of the threatening aspects of black power, it meant much less than that to Negroes. Bayard Rustin, one of the leading analysts of the Negro movement, said, "The truth of the matter is that community control as an idea is provincial and as a program is extremely conservative. It appears radical to some people because it has become the demand around which the frustrations of the Negro community have coalesced."

In a real sense, the demand for community control that was heard so frequently in the late 1960's was a product of the white society, an outgrowth of white goals insofar as black citizens were concerned. Across the complete spectrum of Negro thought there is agreement that the desire for black communities to control their institutions and their future grew out of a bitter realization that for many years to come segregation by one means or another would be a fact of life for millions of Negroes.

For the Harlem welfare mother, it was unrealistic even to think of the possibility of moving to the New Jersey suburbs. For the Negro family in Memphis getting by on $6,000 a year there was no way possible to move to the white suburbs, where not only economic pressures but strong social attitudes of whites prevented such a move. Despite open occupancy laws on the federal, state, and local levels, the typical American city in 1972, through zoning, pricing and other means, made it extremely difficult if not impossible for low-income Negroes to move into white or integrated neighborhoods outside the central city. Across the country, there were overt protests against construction of federally subsidized, low-income housing—projects that would be available to Negroes—in the suburbs.

George Romney, Secretary of Housing and Urban Development in the Nixon Administration, and other officials have acknowledged publicly that the policies of the federal government had much to do with the development of segregated neighborhoods in American cities. Until 1950, the Federal Housing Administration had a policy written into its manuals against insuring homes in integrated neighborhoods. At the same time, through a practice called "redlining," it generally refused to insure loans for housing in the central cities where the masses of Negroes lived on grounds that to do so would constitute a poor risk. These policies, of course, were changed over the years. But as Edward Rutledge, co-director of the National Committee Against Discrimination in Housing, pointed out in testimony to a Senate committee in 1970, "The same people largely remain in FHA and while the policies of the agency have changed, the practices, in many cases, have not."

69

In the building boom that came after World War II, the federal government, then, encouraged the pattern of the white suburban "noose" around the increasingly black central city, a pattern that is now seen in almost every major urban area in the country. The increase in riots and crime in the 1960's sped the migration of whites out of the central cities and they took a large part of their economic base with them. Thus blacks became increasingly isolated from the larger white society and the goal of integration that was pursued with vigor in the early 1960's became much more difficult to achieve. The United States Commission on Civil Rights held hearings around the country and concluded that in cities such as St. Louis and Baltimore most of the jobs were in the suburbs and Negroes were excluded from them by a lack of public transportation, zoning exclusion, high prices of suburban homes, and by the practices of local and federal officials. In the Northern cities there were more segregated schools, due to housing patterns, than had existed in 1954, when the Supreme Court held segregation by law and policy to be unconstitutional.

Under the new policies, Negroes with middle and high incomes were able to some extent to move out of the central cities, and many of them did so, according to preliminary 1970 census figures and several national surveys. But much of the outward movement was believed to be to "ghettolets" (poor black areas developing in the suburbs) and the masses of urban Negroes remained in the central cities.

The blacks, then, were to a large extent bound to their own communities whether they liked it or not. For those who took a realistic view of this, the logical action was to try to obtain as much power and self-control as possible within the white society. Alan A. Altshuler, in a study done for the

Urban Institute and entitled *Community Control: The Black Demand for Participation in Large American Cities*, pointed out that virtually none of the black leaders advocated denying individual blacks the right to move to predominantly white neighborhoods. "All the blacks have done," he wrote, "is to change tactics. They have revived the distinction between integration and equality as objectives, and determined to concentrate for the time being on the latter."

There has been, however, considerable disagreement as to what constitutes community control. The proposals in the last few years have ranged all the way from complete withdrawal of black communities—economically, politically, and socially, as far as possible under the circumstances—to the simple expansion of powers traditionally sought by Negro leaders. These differences have contributed to deep divisions within the Negro community. But virtually all of the plans advocated are a great deal more sophisticated and realistic than the separatist answers supplied in the past by Bishop Turner, Marcus Garvey, and others. There is a general agreement among most Negro leaders, it seems, that there are limits to community control, both as to what it can accomplish and what it promises. Rustin, writing in *Harper's* magazine in January, 1970, had this to say:

For a complex technological society there is no such thing as an autonomous community within a large metropolitan area. Neighborhoods, particularly poor neighborhoods, will remain dependent upon outside suppliers for manufactured goods, transportation, utilities, and other services. There is, for instance, unemployment in the ghetto while the vast majority of new jobs are being created in the suburbs. If black people are to have access to those jobs, there must be a metropolitan transportation system that can carry them to the suburbs cheaply and quickly. Control over the ghetto cannot build such a system nor can it provide jobs within the ghetto.

What the majority of Negro leaders seemed to be seeking, then, was a very limited community control that would enhance the power of blacks, appeal to black pride and self-determination, yet leave the way open for integration into the white society on several different levels.

The two national rights organizations that have most consistently stood for integration, the NAACP and the National Urban League, have formally endorsed community control while rejecting the view that it would lead to separatism. Whitney Young, executive director of the Urban League, said in the summer of 1969, "Community control is the most crucial issue right now. Institutions have failed because control isn't in the hands of the people who live in the communities."

Much of the movement toward community control centered on the efforts of blacks in large cities to have a larger role in running the public schools in their neighborhoods. The NAACP in its 1969 convention adopted a resolution that said:

We strongly support the concept of community control of public schools, particularly in the big-city school systems of the North and West, as a means of achieving fundamental changes in the schools and insuring accountability. . . . We do not believe that community control and desegregation are inherently incompatible or in conflict unless they are made to be by advocates, white or black, of racial separatism.

In this sense, community control has a number of positive aspects that were missing in the various movements for establishment of all-black towns, states, or other political subdivisions. Altshuler wrote of some of these:

The hope of community control is that it might provide a base for long-term reform. It would provide an arena in which blacks might engage their energies and experience power. It would provide a mechanism for transforming the bureaucratic subcultures (by changing their basic lines of political dependence). It would provide a focus for black political organization. It might help to build black skills and self-respect. But most important, it would give blacks a tangible stake in the American political system. By giving them systems they considered their own, it would—hopefully—enhance the legitimacy of the whole system in their eyes.

In the limited sense, Negroes by 1972 already had accomplished a good deal of community control. They had taken over a good percentage of the retail businesses operating in their neighborhoods, businesses that formerly were virtually all white; they had established community organizations that wielded a degree of political and economic power; they elected blacks to numerous public offices, including the mayoralties of such major cities as Cleveland, Newark, Gary, Indiana, and Wichita, Kansas; and they had made considerable progress in some cities toward decentralizing the public school system so that residents in the black neighborhoods would have more say in how the schools were to be run.

In fact, one reason that there was a decline in the large city riots toward the end of the decade was that both radical and moderate Negro leaders counseled against destruction of property on the ground that it would weaken community control. Thomas I. Atkins, Boston's Negro city councilman, said, "People are not going to destroy that which they are about to own."

To a large extent the drive for community control among Negroes was an effort to obtain a degree of the autonomy long enjoyed by many white communities. This was graphically illustrated in the June, 1970, issue of *City* magazine, published by the National Urban Coalition. With an article on decentralization of government, the magazine showed two aerial views, one of the Bedford-Stuyvesant section of New York City, where there has been agitation for community control, and another of spacious, tree-lined streets of a white suburban community having its own metropolitan government and school board but with only a fraction of Bedford-Stuyvesant's population. If Brooklyn's 500-block ghetto of Bedford-Stuyvesant were a city unto itself," the caption said, "it would rank among the 30 most populous in the nation; yet as a section of a borough of a metropolis, its 500,000 residents have virtually none of the direct control over their community's destiny enjoyed by the citizens of a typical suburban community." It was this kind of control, largely, that blacks were seeking.

Altshuler pointed out that of the black leaders and would-be leaders in search of mass followings today:

None believe that the black masses can be mobilized around the remote goal of integration. Popular followings are secured and maintained by focusing on more immediate desires: jobs, physical security, better schools, better housing, more sympathetic treatment from public servants, and so on. They are also secured by establishing cultural rapport: that is, by manipulating the right symbols in the right style. The right style at the present time [1970] is militant revivalist. The right symbols are those which express pride in black, and which attempt to purge traditional black self-hatred by ridiculing the traditional aspiration for acceptance into white America.

All this helps to explain and give impetus to the demands for community control.

7

How Black
Power Works

ONE WAY to come to an understanding of what is involved in the separatism versus integration argument is to take a look at some of the recent proposals that are being made or implemented. One of these that gets quickly to the crux of the matter comes from the Congress of Racial Equality. CORE, it will be remembered, instigated the freedom rides that attacked segregation in public transportation and was a combatant in cities across the country against segregation in every form and practice. The founders of CORE came largely from the Fellowship of Reconciliation, a pacifist-oriented group. It was founded in 1942 in the belief that direct action was needed in the search for racial justice, that the legalism then followed by the NAACP and other moderate organizations was not enough to bring down segregation. Its membership was interracial.

Much of CORE's membership was in Northern cities. With the emergence of black power in the mid-1960's and the entry of many young militants into the ranks of CORE, leaders of the organization found themselves under pressure to stop insisting on integration and reconciliation and seek instead political and economic power for blacks and to discredit nonviolence. James Farmer, who had combined militance with absolute nonviolence, was forced out as national director. He was succeeded by Floyd McKissick, who leaned more to separatism, and within a short period of time McKissick was succeeded by Roy Innis, who leaned all the way. In the process, CORE disintegrated as a national organization but continued under the same name with chapters in a handful of cities, and Innis continued to have some influence as a Negro leader.

Early in 1970, Innis toured the South trying to persuade both blacks and whites to give up the long fight for school integration and adopt instead a plan CORE advocated to decentralize school governing bodies so that the black districts would have their own school boards, the white districts theirs. Under the plan, the tax base would remain the same and the money distributed through the proliferation of school boards on a per capita basis. On his tour, Innis drew considerable support from white segregationists who had been fighting court-ordered integration plans, just as Bishop Turner and his emmisaries almost a century before had been well received by former slave owners who looked with favor on the plan to deport black people to Africa.

There was a certain logic to Innis's argument. The Supreme Court's conclusion in 1954 that separate schools are inherently inferior, Innis said, "is not only spurious on its face but insidiously racist in its implication that black children alone among the different races and groups of the world must mix in order to be equal. Blacks who subscribe to this theory are suffering from self-hatred, the legacy of generations of brainwashing. They have been told—and they believe—that it is exposure to whites in and by itself that makes blacks equal citizens."

The problem, Innis argued, is one of control. Even where there was full integration and where blacks were in the majority the school board remained under white control, he said, and little was done to meet the needs of black pupils. "Blacks who have gone along with integration have done so in search for dignity, but have found humiliation at the end of the rainbow," Innis contended. "They integrate for equality but find they are together but still unequal. They have less control and less influence, if that is possible, than ever before. In short, the integration that blacks are likely to get in most instances, North or South, has proven to be token equality, mere show and pure sham."

As to any stigma attached to attending an all-black school, Innis said that had been destroyed when segregation laws were invalidated. There is a difference in going to a black school by choice and going because the state bars the attendance of blacks in white schools. As to the acknowledged inferiority of most all-black schools, Innis argued that this would end when the black community obtained control and was in a position to provide "a truly equal, truly democratic education for its children." In a paper on the proposal, Innis cited this illustration:

Within Mobile County, Alabama, for example, there is a natural community comprising the Davis Avenue, Toulminville, Bullshead area. This community alone has more students than do many existing school districts throughout the state. The citizens and students in this community happen to be black Americans. The schools attended by the youth from this community have been badly run by the Mobile County school board. For years, the talent and energies of the best citizens of the community have been expended in fighting the school board—but without significant results. This community has many special needs different from those of the general population of Mobile County. A healthy pride and sense of purpose is evident and growing in this community. The educational hopes of the residents, however, are continually frustrated by a school board which has shown no sensitivity to their problems. . . . We contend that it is possible to bring dignity and true equality of opportunity to this community without denying the human and constitutional rights of any other community. . . . It is in the spirit of attempting to avert chaos and establishing harmony that this proposal is presented.

The Innis plan would restrict the school lines within an entire state along "natural community lines"—thus separating to a maximum extent black and white sections—provided that most of the residents of both races are in agreement. Pupils within a district would be assigned to schools on a nonracial basis. The school board would be elected and would select teachers and administrative officers. The district would receive state and federal monies under existing distribution formulas and "the local educational dollar will be directed to each school district on a per student basis."

Even though virtually all black leaders were in agreement with Innis on what white control had done to blacks and black schools, the plan was met with strong and sizable opposition in the black communities, particularly in the South. For one thing, it ignored one of the educational arguments for integrated classrooms. This was the central finding of an extensive study made for the Office of Education in 1966 to determine the extent of segregation in the schools throughout the country and its effect on children. It came to be known as the Coleman Report, for the man who headed it, Dr. James S. Coleman of Johns Hopkins University. Dr.

Coleman found that children in school are more influenced by the other children around them than they are by their teachers, the facilities, or materials used. As the proportion of whites in a school increases, the achievement of students in each racial group increases. The reason: "The higher acievement of all racial and ethnic groups in schools with greater proportions of white students is largely, perhaps wholly, related to effects associated with the student body's educational background and aspirations. This means that the apparent beneficial effect of a student body with a high proportion of white students comes not from racial composition per se, but from the better educational background and higher educational aspirations that are, on the average, found among white students. The effect of the student body environment upon a student's achievement appear to lie in the educational proficiency possessed by that student body, whatever its racial or ethnic composition." In the South, of course, the gap between the educational backgrounds of blacks and whites was particularly pronounced.

But even more than this, many Negro leaders who had long been in the struggle to remove racial barriers believed strongly that whenever blacks were separated the white society would find a way to see that they received the short end of public services, the Innis plan of equal tax distribution notwithstanding. Certainly this had been true in the past. Thus leaders such as Marian Wright Edelman, a civil rights attorney, publicly denounced the Innis plan. They noted that the plan pleased many of the white segregationists who had opposed Negro advancement on a number of levels. Whitney Young of the Urban League remarked, "I don't think we ought to let the white man off the hook that easily." And many white liberals took the same point of view. This did not mean, however, that in the large cities where it appeared there was no way to break up the black schools any time soon that moderate blacks were opposed to decentralization and community control of schools. Here the opinion of black leaders for community control was virtually unanimous.

However, in the South, where integration was a viable proposition and where scores of thousands of Negro children went to school with whites for the first time in the fall of 1970, and in many other areas of the country, it appeared that the vast majority of black leaders and the masses of Negro citizens continued to prefer school integration. Pat Watters, information director for the Southern Regional Council, a biracial organization of Southerners, summarized this view in *The New York Times Magazine*:

> Negro Southerners, by and large, support the Supreme Court's recent integration order [to speed desegregation]. They may be even more disillusioned than Northern black people, but they value education. Many still agree with the preponderance of sociological evidence that integrated experience is a necessary ingredient of education. But beyond that, virtually all know out of their Southern experience that the white power structure will put the most money, the best equipment, where white children go to school— *and they want in.*

Even more complex, and less understood, than black goals in education is the subject generally known as black capitalism. Probably the most certain thing about black capitalism is that there is very little of it. A few years ago, E. Franklin Frazier wrote a book called *Black Bourgeoisie* in which he analyzed the attitudes and values of Negroes who had accumulated some wealth. They were depicted as a small, isolated group that had broken with the cultural tradition of blacks but still were not accepted by the white society. There is evidence that this is changing, to a limited extent, that the black middle class is beginning to identify with the problems of the black masses. But the point here is that the black middle class, in comparison to the white society, has been very small. The means by which Negroes could accumulate wealth have been very limited.

Andrew F. Brimmer, the Negro member of the Federal Reserve Board, once said, "The Negro lives and works in the backwaters and eddies of the national economy. This has been true since he arrived on these shores long before the colonies became a nation." In the 1960's there was some progress away from this state of affairs, which a multitude of scholars have found to be due largely to practices of exclusion by white society. But the homes, buildings, and businesses in the Negro neighborhoods across the country, North and South, still were owned and controlled largely by whites. Thus, so were the jobs that were available to blacks. It was understandable, then, that virtually all Negro rights groups put family income at or near the top of their lists of goals. The purpose was to go beyond opening white-owned businesses and institutions to Negro employment and find ways for Negroes to control a larger share of the economy. Richard M. Nixon acknowledged this need in his 1968 campaign for the Presidency, saying that blacks, like everyone else, wanted and deserved a "piece of the action."

This was being approached from many different directions. The Small Business Administration was making and guaranteeing loans to Negroes to start businesses of their own. Negro banks were springing up around the country, backing black businesses with black deposits. Private foundations were advising and assisting Negroes in economic ventures in a variety of ways.

But so small was the Negro's share of the economy at the beginning of the 1960's that it was generally acknowledged that progress had not been very fast. A number of Negro groups advocating separatism advocated some drastic means. One of these was the National Black Economic Development Conference, a small organization of militants. The conference met in Detroit on April 26, 1969, and drafted what it called a "manifesto to the white Christian Churches and the Jewish Synagogues in the United States of America and all other racist institutions."

"Brothers and Sisters," it began. "We have come from all over the country, burning with anger and despair, not only with the miserable economic plight of our people, but fully aware that the racism on which the Western world was built dominates our lives. There can be no separation of the problems of racism from the problems of our economic, political, and cultural degradation."

The document was filled with threats of violence and revolution. "We live inside the United States, which is the most barbaric country in the world, and we have a chance to help bring this government down," it said. "Racism in the United States is so pervasive in the mentality of whites that only an armed, well-disciplined, black-controlled government can insure the stamping out of racism in this country."

As "colonized people inside the United States," the authors of the document demanded from the Christian churches and Jewish synagogues $500 million in reparations. The demand was brought against religious institutions, the document said, because they had "tremendous wealth" and their membership "has profited [from] and still exploits black people."

"Fifteen dollars for every black brother and sister in the

United States is only a beginning of the reparations due us as a people who have been exploited and degraded, brutalized, killed and persecuted," the authors said. The money, it was explained, would go through the conference for the establishment of a Southern Land Bank to buy land for blacks who wished to establish cooperative farms, black printing industries, television stations, a manpower training center for blacks, a strike fund for blacks, a black university, and other institutions.

The Black Manifesto, as it came to be known, would have attracted little attention had not James Forman, one of the organizers of the conference, brought it to public attention in a dramatic manner. On May 4, 1969, he interrupted the services at New York's Riverside Church, a liberal, Protestant body of some material means, took over the pulpit, and presented the Manifesto as the congregation and pastor looked on in disbelief. This was the beginning of a national furor. Forman, who had formerly been a civil rights leader in the South, one of the chief officers of the Student Nonviolent Coordinating Committee, went to conventions and other meetings of various denominations and enunciated the demands. Along the way the price was raised to $3 billion.

It was difficult to understand how anyone not already conscience-stricken by the amply demonstrated facts of racism and racial injustice could have been brought around by the Manifesto. Nevertheless, there was a sizable positive response to the demand. It became a point of prolonged debate in a number of church bodies. Black clergymen within the white denominations generally supported it to some degree. During the following year the conference received almost $300,000 from various churches. Many who did not give to the conference made donations to other Negro groups, the total pledges coming to millions of dollars. Riverside Church, alone, pledged $450,000 over a three-year period for work among the poor, a direct response to the Manifesto. The conference planned to organize a nationwide community organization program in black areas, to purchase a radio station in Lorain, Ohio, and launch several newspapers to promulgate black unity.

There was no way for an outsider to know precisely the motives of Forman and other militants who formed the Black Economic Development Conference. Certainly they would not under any circumstances be advocates of the American political and economic systems as now constituted. But almost everyone who has followed the black movements of late is aware that there is a level of rhetoric and a level of reality. Talk of revolution and violence coming after American cities were damaged by civil disorders has had the effect of frightening some white people who otherwise have been oblivious to the needs of blacks. Perhaps in the Black Manifesto, then, there is not as much sentiment for violence and separatism as there is language that might move, to some extent, those in control. The chairman of the conference in 1970 was the Reverend Calvin B. Marshall, III, pastor of the Varick Memorial Church in Brooklyn, who keeps a picture of Martin Luther King on the wall of his office.

The black protest of the late 1960's and early 1970's seemed to be shaped for its time. After all, it has been almost one hundred years since Bishop Turner, the black militant of his day, tried to escape oppression by moving Negroes back to Africa. Since then black activists have become increasingly sophisticated in their methods. For the most part they know there is no escape to Africa, or to any other country. But they know there are ways that the American system can be moved, if they only put their minds to it.

There has been confusion, too, about what blacks are seeking in politics. The black power doctrine, as enunciated by Stokely Carmichael, Charles V. Hamilton, and others held that in organizing and operating politically blacks should avoid coalitions with whites except when the blacks define the terms of the coalition and are operating from a position of strength. The basis of this belief was that the whites with whom blacks had been forming coalitions, largely liberal Democrats, were so much a part of the white society that had subordinated blacks that they could not be trusted to represent the best interests of blacks. Blacks, even militants, are still forming coalitions with whites. In many areas they are integrated into the predominantly Democratic parties. But black politics, nevertheless, has moved a long way in the direction advocated by the black power advocates. Generally it has not been a radical change, only a shifting of position to add more leverage to the black vote. Look at a few examples.

In Philadelphia, a group of black professionals and community leaders formed the Black Political Forum. The Democratic Party in that city, as in most, has been heavily populated by blacks. Philadelphia has a black Congressman, Robert N. C. Nix, and several black members in the state legislature. There are blacks in the city government and in the judiciary. Yet the organizers of the forum felt that the Democratic Party was not the most effective political vehicle for the city's Negroes. Willie W. Goode, one of the organizers explained the reasons in an interview in his office in the spring of 1970. "The whole issue," he said, "is that those who blacks elect to office wind up not being responsible to the people but to the party. When the machine picks them as candidates they are as good as in, so they answer to the machine, not to the people. And the machine is controlled by whites."

The forum had a long way to go. It was in the first stages of formation, and challenging the Democratic Party in Philadelphia was a big order. But Goode did not anticipate a total confrontation. Candidates representing the forum would be free to participate in the Democratic primaries and if elected would work with the Democratic Party up to the national level. It boiled down to whether "the machine" or black leaders picked the candidates who would make the best showing in the primaries. In that sense, the forum was not separatist but more Democratic. It would put power at a level closer to the people. And it was a device to give blacks a little more leverage in power than they already had.

There were other examples of this across the country. In Alabama, Orzell Billingsley, a civil rights attorney of Birmingham, was leading a movement to incorporate into municipalities black settlements scattered throughout the state. These settlements have come under county governments, run by whites, have had neither municipal charter nor services. One of the largest of these was Roosevelt City, population 4,500. It is, in fact, a suburban community between Birmingham and Bessemer. Many of its residents work in the nearby steel mills or other industries. Yet a large part of the population is exceedingly poor and the unemployment rate is chronically high. None of the surrounding municipalities, all white run, wanted to incorporate Roosevelt City. Racial considerations aside, the cost of providing police and fire protection, water and sewerage services would far exceed the amount received in taxes.

The community in 1968 qualified as an incorporated municipality under the laws of Alabama. The first order of business was the election of a mayor and city council. Freddie C. Rodgers, the mayor, explained to a reporter in the spring of 1970 what it was all about. Simply by becoming a city, he said, two things were accomplished. First, the people of the community, all Negroes, achieved community control and a larger role in the politics of the area. Under the Jefferson County government, Roosevelt City could not elect one of its own to a policy-making position. County-wide blacks were outnumbered by whites who had shown no inclination to share control with blacks. Under incorporation, Roosevelt City had its own government and its elected officials had a voice in the various councils of government in the area.

The second thing accomplished was that Roosevelt City became eligible for federal assistance that was not flowing to it through the county government. Without federal assistance, Roosevelt City probably could not have raised the revenue needed to give residents even the most basic of city services. Immediately after incorporations, the new government began applying for every federal grant available. The federal dollars began to come in. A $211,000 community center was soon under construction and the city had a commitment for 90 percent of a $400,000 sewer system. Other grants and revenue from local taxes provided for police and fire departments and other services. And there was even some money from the state of Alabama that Roosevelt City as a municipality was eligible to draw.

"Roosevelt City is all-black at the present time," Mayor Rodgers said, "but we are not promoting segregation. The first ordinance we passed was for open housing. We welcome whites. We are showing what poor people can do by pulling together. Once the poor whites see the things that Negroes are doing here that will bring us closer together. I have had some people say to me that what we are doing is hurting the drive for integration. I say to them that I am helping integration. As the mayor of Roosevelt City I integrated the Alabama Municipal Association."

It was that way in many black activities across the country. That which had the appearance of separatism turned out on closer examination to be pragmatism, an effort by a minority to make limited power more effective.

8

Climbing
the Mountain

ON LABOR DAY weekend of 1970, three black groups purporting to be at the forefront of what had come to be called the black revolution met simultaneously in three widely separated locations in the United States. In a sense, they represented both the unity and the divisions that had taken place in the Negro movement since the decline of the nonviolent tradition in the mid-1960's. If the polls are to be believed none of these meetings represented the thinking of the majority of America's 22 million black people. For all pointed, as Thomas A. Johnson wrote in *The New York Times*, toward an ethnic nationalism of one kind or another. But they did contain the thinking of probably a majority of the black activists in the country, and particularly the young who will mold opinions for the future. It may be helpful, therefore, to examine briefly what was said and done at those meetings.

Leaders of the Black Panther Party, those not in jail, dead, impoverished, or exiled, met in Philadelphia—a faction that probably would have been too obscure and small to have attracted national attention had it not been constantly involved in skirmishes with the police in cities across the country. The Panthers had had in a very short time an interesting and tumultuous history. In a sense, it grew out of the Student Nonviolent Coordinating Committee and the Committee's turn to black power in 1966. The first Black Panther Party was in Lowndes County, Alabama, where Stokely Carmichael and other SNCC leaders tried, unsuccessfully, to elect blacks to county offices. As SNCC splintered away in the ideological warfare of those years, many of its leaders moved from the South to the black slums of Northern cities trying to organize a people's movement.

The Black Panthers, however, attracted little attention until May 2, 1967, when twenty-six Panthers armed with loaded shotguns, rifles, and pistols marched into the California state legislature during debate on gun-control legislation. Security guards seized the weapons, unloaded them, and returned them to the Panthers, who then walked out of the building. Not a shot was fired. But public attention was focused on the Black Panther Party for Self-Defense, one of the scattered Panther groups, which had been organized in Oakland, California. Huey P. Newton was the founder and Minister of Self-Defense. The black cat was the party's symbol, Newton explained, because "it is not in the panther's nature to strike first; but when he is backed into a corner, he will respond viciously and wipe out the aggressor."

According to Newton, blacks were held in the central cities "in colonial bondage" by a white society that used the police as an "occupying army" to suppress the population. Panthers would in "self-defense," he said, kill the "pig enforcers" of the colonial system. The Panthers proclaimed themselves to be revolutionaries as well as holders of the "black power concept devised by SNCC. But a program adopted by the party in 1966 showed that the Panthers, in fact, were clinging to the American tradition rather than reaching for an African one, as separatists from Bishop Turner to Elijah Muhammad had done. The program listed ten things the Panthers wanted: freedom, full employment, decent housing, education, exemption from military service, an end to police brutality, freedom of imprisoned blacks, trial by all-black jury, and a "United Nations-supervised plebiscite to be held throughout the black colony in which only black colonial subjects will be allowed to participate, for the purpose of determining the will of black people as to their national destiny."

Then, the program used exact language from the United States Declaration of Independence to proclaim a state of revolution:

We hold these truths to be self-evident, that all men are created equal; that they are endowed by their Creator with certain unalienable rights; that among these are life, liberty, and the pursuit of happiness. That, to secure these rights, governments are instituted among men, deriving their just powers from the consent of the governed; that, whenever any form of government becomes destructive of these ends, it is the right of the people to alter or to abolish it, and to institute a new government, laying its foundation on such principles, and organizing its powers in such form, as to them shall seem most likely to effect their safety and happiness. Prudence, indeed, will dictate that governments long established should not be changed for light and transient causes; and, accordingly, all experience hath shown, that mankind are more disposed to suffer, while evils are sufferable, than to right themselves by abolishing the forms to which they are accustomed. But, when a long train of abuses and usurpations, pursuing invariably the same object, evinces a design to reduce them under absolute despotism, it is their right, it is their duty, to throw off such government, and to provide new guards for their future security.

To solidify their support in the black community, the Panthers instituted a number of community programs. They fed breakfast to school children—in Chicago, they claimed to be giving hot breakfasts to more than three thousand children. Free health clinics were opened in several cities. Panther ideology changed in the process. They began shifting their emphasis from talk about guns and fighting the police to revolutionary propaganda. The Panthers also abandoned the black power doctrine against forming coalitions with whites. Their leaders proclaimed that they had "purged themselves of racism" and were no longer involved in a race war, but in "class struggle." They sought to make coalitions with poor whites, even though there was little evidence of progress. They did succeed in forming coalitions with elements of the New Left, the radical whites. Eldridge Cleaver, Huey Newton, and Bobby Seale, three of the Panther leaders, became heroes of white radical students.

Still, the Panthers might have dwindled away virtually unnoticed had they not been kept constantly before the public eye because of repeated clashes with the police. This followed a pattern almost anyone familiar with the American scene might have predicted. The Panthers laid up arms and made threatening noise against the police and the country and entered into a revolutionary pact with the most extreme elements of the New Left. The police across the country raided Panther headquarters. There was an increase in sniper attacks on police officers. There were more police raids. Panthers and police were killed. Some of the raids appeared to be without any constitutional restraint. In one Chicago raid it appeared that Fred Hampton, Illinois chairman of the Panthers, was fatally shot while sleeping. Black moderates who had no use for Panther methods rallied to their support in protest of police action. Booker Griffin stated the case in the Los Angeles *Sentinel:*

Some say that the Panthers are revolutionaries and do not deserve protection of American civil liberties. I say that George Wallace is a revolutionary and police give him full support. In fact, the Panthers and the Wallacites are opposite sides of the same coin in terms of advocating extreme and literal interpretations of the Constitutional principles of the Republic; Wallacites to serve white supremacy and Panthers to serve black liberation. When Panthers break defined laws, the police have a right to deal with them according to the procedures of the law. In the same instance, the police must not break the law themselves. I submit that were the Panthers to evaporate a new group would soon rise in the community to protest police practices.

So the Panthers became something more to Negroes across the country than the small splinter group they were. At the same time it was apparent that they lacked the substance to attract the mass following of, say, a Bishop Turner or a Marcus Garvey. Their philosophy was both naïve and fatalistic. At the Philadelphia meeting, the Panthers, in their search for coalitions, invited members of the Women's and Gay Liberation Movements to take part. This highly unusual gathering was called the Revolutionary People's Constitutional Convention.

White radicals came and dominated the dialogue on revolutionary ideology. Observers of the scene said the Panther delegates seemed to be intent on displaying their masculine defiance of "the system," a posturing that recalled the succinct analysis of the Panther movement by Dr. J. Alfred

Cannon, a Negro psychiatrist at the University of California in Los Angeles. The Panthers, he said, "consider themselves young warriors—a positive identification which is directly opposed to the image of the Negro male as passive and lazy." In a sense, the Panthers seemed to be authentic American innocents. Like Bishop Turner they had given up on white America, but they saw no chance to gain freedom by escaping to Africa. "We stand," said the Panthers' Minister of Education, Raymond (Masai) Hewitt, "on the principle that the choice for black people is not the choice between life and death, but whether we die fighting or submitting."

There was no indication that the masses of American Negroes were ready to die. They sought, probably as never before, a full measure of life and a number of their moderate leaders were concerned that the Panthers might start a shooting war with whites that would bring more and more repression on the black community. Even a Muslim spokesman said, "If you don't have the power to do, don't have the mouth to say." And there was criticism of the Panthers from blacks who were seeking separatism for forming coalitions and working with whites. "White cooperation is white co-option," had become the byword in the separatist movement of the late 1960's and in 1970. There was no clearer exponent of this than the Congress of Racial Equality, which assembled five hundred delegates in Mobile while the Panthers were meeting in Philadelphia.

The CORE convention, led by Roy Innis, sought not only the school plan that Innis had been promoting through the South but also "black control" of the "instruments of power" as they affect the black community. This boiled down to decentralization of almost every instrument of government so that black neighborhoods would have the chief policy-making voice in the police, social services, and education. In addition, the black neighborhoods would have more investment and control in the economy. What CORE was pushing was the concept of community control that had been gaining favor among blacks for several years. It was hard to judge how much support the CORE concept had in black communities across the country. It was evident, however, that even though community control was generally desired, great numbers of Negroes, undoubtedly the majority, were unwilling to segregate themselves to achieve the kind of power Innis was seeking for blacks. Even while CORE was meeting, hundreds of thousands of blacks throughout the South were entering integrated schools, an achievement they had long been seeking.

An indication of the complexity involved, however, was the fact that Innis left his Mobile meeting for a time and joined the third black conference, held in Atlanta. This was the largest conference, the most diverse, and perhaps the most significant in terms of defining black goals. The Congress of African People attracted more than 2,500 delegates, including a sprinkling of Mexican-Americans, Puerto Ricans, and blacks from Africa and the West Indies. A number of American delegates wore African dress. The purpose was to stress black unity, to point the way for building black institutions, and to build alliances between black people around the world. They called it "Pan-Africanism" and "nation building."

A large number of the delegates were community workers and college students. Almost everyone there supported the belief that whites who wish to help blacks could be of the most service by seeking to change white society. There was some support for building alliances with friendly white groups, but there was more concern for reaching the masses of Negroes who had not been touched by the trend toward black pride and unity. One of the speakers was a long-time integrationist, Whitney Young of the National Urban League. He told the delegates that he continued to favor integration but added, "I make no apologies at all for attending a conference where only blacks are. We are a family and it is appropriate and essential that family members get together before they plan to go elsewhere."

Many of the leaders of the conference had been active in the nonviolent movement of the 1960's and were now searching for new ways to help the Negro cause. There was Chester Lewis of Wichita, Kansas, who had been a member of the board of directors of the National Association for the Advancement of Colored People. The chairman was Haywood Henry, Jr., twenty-seven-year-old candidate for a Ph.D. at Boston University who had participated in demonstrations for integration in his early youth. Henry described himself as a nationalist but he pointed up how far removed this brand of nationalism was from that preached by Marcus Garvey when he said, "The relevant question for blacks is liberation, not separation or integration."

Not separation or integration but liberation. That had become the popular slogan in a large segment of the black community. Fashion advertisements for blacks proclaimed "the liberated look." *Ebony* magazine, which has been identified with the middle class but which, like the black middle class itself, has become increasingly concerned about social issues and the problems of poor blacks, devoted an entire issue in August, 1970, to the debate over Negro goals. It covered the spectrum of opinion—from Elijah Muhammad to Roy Wilkins.

The lead article was written by Lerone Bennett, Jr., the senior editor and author of several books on black goals. Trying to decide between integration and separation was "abstract, false and diversionary," he maintained. "No other group has been forced to expend needed energies endlessly debating a false issue which was designed to hide them from themselves." True integration, he said, is a two-way street in which both sides give and take, but whites have proved over again they do not want to give.

"A few years ago," he said by way of example, "I spoke to a group of white radical ministers who complained about the 'self-segregation' of blacks. They told me that blacks were not playing fair, adding, 'They will not abandon their churches and integrate with us.' I told those ministers that, in my opinion, the best Baptist church in Atlanta, Ga., was pastored by Martin Luther King, Jr. They agreed. I then suggested that all white Baptists in Atlanta, Ga., should leave their inferior second-class white churches and integrate into the mainstream of Martin Luther King's church. Their mouths came open in amazement. In their innocence, in their racism, it had never occurred to them that integration would cost *them* anything."

Both integrationists and separatists are too much concerned with the limits prescribed by whites, Bennett wrote, and blacks need a philosophy that rises above this:

The philosophy of liberation calls for a transcendence of the either/or dilemma which has had such a disastrous impact on African-American policy. The liberationist concedes the power of the integrationist's dream but points out that black power is necessary to accomplish it. He concedes the desirability of some African-Americans returning to Africa but says that most African-Americans are going to triumph or die here. He estimates there are more than 100 million people of African descent in the New World; and he says that the historical task of these people, who can *never* go home again en masse, is to link up with the Indians, the disadvantaged and the alienated and assimilate instead of being assimilated. To adopt and change the meaning of a statement William Strickland made in another connection: If every African takes care of business wherever he is, then every place will be a correct place for Africans.

In a real sense, the cry for "liberation" was not much different from the slogan used in the nonviolent movement, "Do you want your freedom?" But it was tempered by the experiences of the 1960's and the limits that blacks believed had been demonstrated to them. It did not, as the nonviolent movement did, assume that the white society could be persuaded to accept blacks on an equal basis. But neither did it call for the building of barriers or the fleeing into black enclaves, as the separatists had prescribed. It did not call for the $200-a-week machinist to quit working at General Motors because that corporation is white controlled. It did not deny the importance of the long struggle against segregation. What it sought most was the building of group power in the way that the Irish, the Jews, the Poles, and the Italians have done in this country.

In the process of all this, black attitudes have become enormously complex, so much so that Bennett, and others, indicated that a public opinion poll would be hard pressed to measure the "integrationist" or "separatist" sentiment. "Most blacks are integrationists and separationists and pluralists—all at the same time," Bennett wrote. "They are 'integrationists' on Monday morning when they go downtown to meet the 'man,' 'separationists' when they return to the black community on Monday night, 'integrationists' on

Wednesday night when they go downtown to the movies, 'separationists' on Saturday night when they go to an all-black bar. . . . pluralists on Sunday morning when they go to the African Methodist or Pearly Grove Baptist. . . . There is an antinomy here. Blacks love America with a love that is full of hate, and they hate America with a hate that is full of love."

The idea of pluralism that has been gaining in the black community was expressed by the Reverend Jesse L. Jackson, an aide to Martin Luther King and director of Operation Breadbasket, a movement that seeks jobs and food for blacks on the South Side of Chicago. "The idea of America being a melting pot where everyone is assimilated is wrong," he said in an interview. "America is more like a bowl of vegetable soup with Irish, Italians, Poles, blacks and all representing peas, corn, carrots and tomatoes, and the common base is the continent of North America. The trouble is that the blacks have been pushed to the bottom. Well, what we're saying is that we are going to come to the top and be recognized, or we are going to turn the bowl over."

Jackson, still personally committed to nonviolence, does not deny, as some blacks attempt to do, that there is a wide diversity in the black community that makes unity extremely difficult. Bayard Rustin, writing in *Harper's* magazine in January, 1970, on "The Failure of Black Separatism," said:

The fact is that like every other racial or ethnic group in America, Negroes are divided by age, class, and geography. Young Negroes are at least as hostile toward their elders as white New Leftists are toward their liberal parents. They are in addition separated by vast gaps in experience, Northern from Southern, urban from rural. And even more profound are the disparities in wealth among them. In contrast to the white community, where the spread of income has in recent years remained unchanged or has narrowed slightly, economic differentials among blacks have increased. In 1965, for example, the wealthiest 5 percent of white and nonwhite families received 15.5 percent of the total income in their respective communities. In 1967, however, the percentage of white income received by the top 5 percent of white families had dropped to 14.9 percent while among nonwhites the share of income of the top 5 percent of the families had risen to 17.5 percent. This trend probably reflects the new opportunities which are available to black professionals in industry, government, and academia, but have not touched the condition of lower-class and lower-middle-class Negroes.

Rustin had said a couple of years earlier that the fundamental mistake the black nationalist movement made was that it did not comprehend that class is a greater driving force than color and that any effort to build a society that is based on color alone was doomed. This was when blacks were going through their most intense anti-white period. As Jesse Jackson described his own experience, "First, I was hung up on whites, then I went through an anti-white, pro-black period, and now whites being around don't threaten me because I have self-confidence."

Rustin described the process as a rebellion against the inferior position in which blacks had long been held. "While rebelling there is rejection of those who used to be loved most," Rustin said in 1968. "Every teen-ager has to go through hating mother and father, precisely because he loves them. Now he's got to make it on his own. Thus, Martin Luther King and A. Philip Randolph and Roy Wilkins and Bayard Rustin and all the people who marched in the streets are all 'finks' now. And the liberals, and the Jews who have done most among the liberals, are also told to get the hell out of the way."

There was, in 1970, much of this still in the air. The drive for "liberation" contained a degree of naïveté in its insistence that blacks ignore the attitudes of the controlling white society in forming their strategies and philosophies. But a maturing process had taken place. This could be seen in tours of United States cities taken by *New York Times* reporters in the spring of 1969, and again in 1970.

Interviews with hundreds of people in the black neighborhoods of the large cities showed that, considering the diversity and differences in ideology, a remarkable unity had taken place. From Philadelphia to Seattle the word was out that black did not attack black, as had been common everywhere in the mid-1960's. "We realize," said a militant young street worker in Chicago, "that to build the black nation a lot of us have to do different things. The NAACP is doing their thing and the Panthers are doing theirs and you don't hear them fighting with each other." Everywhere there was ferment and action by the cadre of community workers that had been created through the combination of the civil rights movement and federal and local anti-poverty programs. It was not unusual to find a black activist with an eighth-grade education who knew more about the intricacies of the federal grant programs than some of the officials in Washington who administered them. And there was an understanding that each was contributing in his own way to a better day for blacks.

President Kennedy, when he was trying to make peace with Southern politicians and push civil rights at the same time, said, "The things that divide us are not as great as those which unite us." Black leaders seemed to be saying pretty much the same thing. Martin Luther King was the leader of the frequently scorned nonviolent movement, but more than two years after his death he was, nevertheless, the chief hero of blacks throughout the country, militants as well as moderates. Addison Gayle, Jr., in a series of essays published under the title *The Black Situation,* wrote a definition of black power that a wide spectrum of the black community could agree to:

What Black Power means for many Negroes is a repudiation of the values, morals and ethics of a white majority. Black power means an exploration of black culture; and the realization that within this culture are those values which a black minority can, without shame embrace. . . . *More significantly, however, Black Power is a creative concept aimed at destroying one hundred years of mental enslavement, distorted images, and meaningless clichés . . . a rebuke to white experts who do not realize that to be black in America is to journey through the fiery labyrinthine corridors of hell* [emphasis added].

The black community leaders encountered on the urban tours were on the whole articulate, and they had something to say. One would not expect to find eloquence on the racial struggle inside the administration building of the Detroit School Board. But there it was in Arthur L. Johnson, a long-time civil rights leader who had been hired to coordinate civil rights enforcement in the schools. To Johnson, the Negro movement had been a long struggle for dignity, recognition, and a decent life and he believed that black rage that had found its outlet in violence was beginning to be channeled into traditional or radical politics that was intended to disarm the American system and impel it to change. And, in a sense, he believed it was beginning to work.

"The assertion of black power involves, in both a psychological and a political sense, a new independence and expression of self-worthiness," he said. "Real political power is achieved as a result. Second, a great many white people now recognize that they can't look at black people the way they used to any more. There is a growing awareness in the white majority that it can't be as callous to black people as it used to be.

"It's natural for people to resist changes until finally they get to a period of resignation," he added. "We aren't there yet, but we're getting there. What has distorted the picture is the black trend toward separatism. It's a good thing in developing racial pride and unity, but it ought not to go to an extreme."

But Johnson, in a one-hour interview in his office, returned time and again to what he called the persistence of the black revolt. "There is so much sadness in the black family," he said. "If you have any feeling left, you can't but be burdened with the tragedy of it. It should come as no surprise when well-trained middle-class blacks come out fighting now."

Leader after leader left the clear impression that, whatever was said, the goal was to move the system to a change that could accommodate the new black aspirations, even though there was a general feeling in the black community that the country was, at least temporarily, moving to the right, as indicated by the policies of the Nixon Administration. In University City, Missouri, a suburb of St. Louis, Jack Kirkland, the only black member of the school board, had been defeated in a try for reelection because he and his white running mates had favored a plan that would move the generally liberal college community from partial to complete school integration. Kirkland, who lived in an integrated neighborhood, was not embittered by the experience, but he was saddened. He said:

If it [integration] can't work here, we really are talking about separate societies, about coexistence. And coexistence ultimately ends up in confrontation. My own feelings are that it's not possible to have a society that has a very strong right and a very strong left. Unless there's a radical group for the middle, then there's no hope for our society. I can't afford the luxury of licking wounds and leaving the fight to the next guy. There are no winners in a completely polarized society, only losers. We have to recruit more people to understand that. I'm not talking about a silent majority. I'm talking about an articulate, militant majority, working on behalf of the principles enunciated many years ago.

There was in the spring of 1970 even more emphasis than there had been the year before on black pride and consciousness but less demand, it seemed, for separatism of the kind sought by radical groups here and there—those who sought colonies in Africa and separate states—than there had been immediately following the riots of 1967 and 1968.

There was increasing talk of "short-range separatism" under which blacks would build economic and social institutions in preparation for eventual integration in the larger society. For example, Dunbar S. McLaurin, a black economist, argued that emerging black businesses are "now much too frail to compete successfully directly within the economy. They must be sheltered, and nurtured. . . . It is as much a transitional and preparatory stage as the period of time a child is sheltered within the home and the schools before he is sent out to compete in the world as an adult." But what this really came back to was community control, of sorts, and here again the emphasis was almost always put on the pluralist tradition of America. No matter how one looked at the matter, it almost always came out as another means of assuming a share of America and nudging the country to adjust to black experience.

One of the most militant and articulate spokesmen for separatism was Imamu Amiri Baraka, better known as the writer LeRoi Jones. Baraka was one of the most controversial supporters of Kenneth A. Gibson in his successful race for mayor of Newark in 1970. He was outspoken throughout the campaign and later when he was opposing the teachers' union in the prolonged school strike in Newark in 1971. Baraka's pronouncements seemed a long way from the conciliatory preachments that had prevailed in the nonviolent movement, but a closer examination of what he was saying showed him, too, to be seeking traditional American goals. During the teachers' strike, for example, he wrote, "We are out to protect our children and raise the quality of education in the city. We are not coming out to Short Hills, West Orange, Livingston, etc., trying to control the educational process of predominantly white communities. We are trying to help shape the education of our children, just as any self-respecting parents anywhere would want to do. White people tend to call this 'separatism' when black people and Puerto Ricans are involved, but no one is going anywhere. We simply want the power to control the 'space' we are in, not just geographic, but institutional, political and economic."

This, of course, did not answer the question of what would happen to whites in Newark if leaders like Baraka should gain the kind of control they sought. Would the whites enjoy the civil liberties and opportunities long denied to blacks? That remained an open question because hardly anywhere, certainly not in Newark, had blacks gained geographic, institutional, political, and economic control. It was still the white man's country, and the nationalists chiefly were seeking power wherever they could find it.

To be sure, there was an increase in terrorism in the central cities, more policemen being shot without direct provocation and more random bombing of buildings and other facilities. But this was the radical fringe that had split farther and farther from the center. And there was militancy on the rise among the young and in many of the black neighborhoods there were indications that robbery, theft, and assault against whites had become a form of social protest. But a greater threat to order probably came from white radicals, who also were a fringe group but greater in numbers because they came from the majority race. Blacks who really wanted a sudden overturning of the society so that something new and different could be built were looking to white radical youths to do the job. In Detroit one night in 1970, a black radical who had grown weary of trying to achieve changes "through the system," turned to a middle-aged white reporter and said, "Blacks are not going to tear this country down, it's going to be the white kids, your sons and daughters."

Making up much of the base of the Negro population is what has been described as the "silent black majority," members of the working class who have an entirely different viewpoint about life and goals and the country than the black activists and intellectuals who have attracted most of the attention. Charles V. Hamilton described some of the characteristics of these in *The New York Times Magazine* in the summer of 1970. He made it clear that their political beliefs are not to be confused with those of the white silent majority. They do not want a period of "benign neglect" of minority needs and they believe the Vietnam policy is wrong, Hamilton wrote. They do not view the police as pigs but neither do they see them as protectors of the black community. They work hard, send their children to Sunday school, and endeavor to get them into college. Their culture is not a permissive one. Hamilton described their attitudes about Negro goals:

They are not nearly as dogmatic on race issues as the popular literature and many of their spokesmen would have one believe. They are supporters of "black power" and "integration" at the same time. . . . By "black power" they mean, "we've got to learn to stick together like the Jews and stand up for our rights." By "integration" they mean overcoming racial discrimination. They are not intimately familiar with the debate between the Black Panthers and the black cultural nationalists over Marxism. And if asked if they believe in "working with whites," their first reaction is to understand this to refer to "on the job," not "in the movement."

In many ways this group reacts to the Black Panthers in much the way it reacted to the Black Muslims and to other highly visible black organizations with a reputation for "militancy." That is, these organizations represent many of the feelings but not the sense of feasibility of the masses of blacks. To the extent that the Panthers speak and act "boldly" their courage and forthrightness are admired. Their breakfast programs are applauded and are seen as "worthwhile"; their goal of revolution is seen as "unrealistic" and "idealistic." Their bravado is unimpressive and is viewed as "mind-blowing," intended largely for whites—especially the guilty and self-conscious ones.

A further indication that blacks were seeking a traditional minority position in American life came in 1971 and 1972, when black activists across the country turned to the political processes. The aim, it seemed from many sources, was to build a national black political movement that would seek not black nationalism, but leverage for Negroes to break out of the cycle of poverty and rejection. Some saw in it a revival of "the dream" that Martin Luther King talked of so frequently.

The chief manifestation of this was the dramatic emergence on the national scene of the Black Congressional Caucus, an organization and action group composed of the Negro members of the House of Representatives. Walter E. Fauntroy, one of the thirteen caucus members in 1971, the nonvoting delegate from the District of Columbia and a former aide to Dr. King, found a direct connection between the defunct nonviolent movement led by Dr. King and the move to politics. "After Selma and the Voting Rights Act of 1965," he said in a speech, "we were going to concentrate on politics. After all, the act brought one million new black registrations in the South and it was natural that we would move in that direction. But then there was the Vietnam war and somehow we let that and other things sidetrack us. Now, the political movement has come, nevertheless, and we are pursuing it everywhere."

The political movement thus continues and gives continuity to the ancient effort of American Negroes to seek their freedom through legitimate means and to use that freedom, as each individual desires, to pursue the same goals that other Americans have sought and achieved. The Congressional Black Caucus, and other black political coalitions, works like most pressure groups in the United States. At the Caucus' first annual fund-raising dinner in Washington in the summer of 1971, the ballroom was integrated, so much so that corporations like General Motors and the Great Atlantic and Pacific Tea Company bought tables for $2,400 apiece. The Caucus set up a staff and performs a variety of services for blacks, ranging from putting pressure on white members of Congress for legislation that would help blacks to holding public hearings on discrimination in the armed services.

And so it goes. Behind almost every paradox of the situation was another segment of the black population seeking to employ the American system just as segments of the majority had for generations. Charles S. Brown, an executive of the Inner City Business Improvement Forum, a black-owned economic development corporation in Detroit, expressed in an interview, perhaps as accurately as anyone else, how it was with the masses of Negroes in America as a new decade got under way.

"As Dr. King said," he remarked, "you have to keep trying to climb the mountain. Hard as it is. The great, astounding quality of the black American is his perseverance. The hostiles say it's a hoax. 'Don't try to build it,' they say. 'Tear it down.' The Panthers say 'genocide.' But the mass of black Americans get up every morning and pursue the American dream. The day that black America stops persevering—the day they give up—that will be the black day."

9

What Lies Ahead

IT IS IMPOSSIBLE for a white person to put himself in the place of a black and to make a judgment about what the goals of blacks should be. Whites should not even try. It is possible, however, for an observer of any color to look at the empirical evidence and make a judgment about the interplay between various peoples within the overall society. Whatever thread of objective analysis one wishes to follow, it almost always leads to the conclusions of the Kerner Commission made early in 1968 as the urban riots were about to reach their peak and as two national leaders—Martin Luther King, Jr., and Robert F. Kennedy—were about to be assassinated. The Kerner Commission concluded that separate hostile camps established on the basis of race violate both the promise and the possibility of America and are destined for failure; that men of all persuasions and color should be free to move, if they wish, throughout the society so long as the civil liberties of others are not violated in the process; and that all should be free to establish communities based on common interests and culture in the tradition of American pluralism that has flourished and nourished minorities for generations.

After long experience, much of it bitter, there are now certain things that we know. We know that all-black communities composed predominantly of the poor and ignorant and cut off from the commerce and culture of the country at large decay and fester; we have seen this in all-black towns of the South and we have seen it in public housing and tenements of the North.

We know that black capitalism is at best exceedingly slow and does not necessarily promise relief for the poor even after a large black middle class has been established.

We know that the children of any poor minority do better in school when most of their classmates come from homes with strong educational backgrounds; the Coleman Report and other studies have shown that to be true.

We know that unemployment and welfare dependency rise in communities separated by considerable distances from the economic base controlled by the majority; we have seen this happen to people in the central cities as whites have migrated to the suburbs, taking the factories, the banks, and the supermarkets with them.

We know that all manner of misconceptions and ill-founded distrust arises when groups of sharply differing background, culture, and wealth isolate themselves from one another; we have seen this in the white suburbs, where there is little understanding of what black people are all about; we have seen it in the inner-city slums, where some black children grow up believing that anyone with white skin is evil.

We know that a declaration of violence on the part of a minority as a means of gaining freedom and equality brings more ills in the long run than gains in the short run, just as repression of a minority by the majority reaps affliction for everyone.

We should know by now that blacks and whites in this country need each other. Whites have the wealth, education, and resources still lacking in much of the black community. Recent economic gains made by blacks did not begin to close the gap between black and white. Blacks bring to the society a spiritual dimension that white America lacks and needs; anyone who followed Martin Luther King's crusades or has known black people intimately know that this is true.

I believe that the majority of blacks have known all this all along, as the preceding chapters have indicated. If this is true, it reinforces the conclusion of the Kerner Commission that the chief burden for change rests on the white majority. The commission said that blacks must have the same choice that has always been open to whites—to have their own settlements, in the honored tradition of pluralism, or to move out into the society at large. It is with the latter choice that the failures of American society are most apparent. The suburbs, to many blacks, are as hostile as the armed camp of the enemy, despite an array of civil rights laws and national policy that denounces discrimination.

The Kerner Commission said that the majority must simultaneously open the suburbs and their vast opportunities for employment, services, and education to blacks and put considerable resources into making the inner cities livable. Neither has been done in the massive way that the commission recommended, and we have seen increased hostilities and polarization and lately the beginnings of guerrilla warfare. When both are done, and the blacks see that the majority is acting in good faith, I believe that violence will decline, organizations such as the Panthers will diminish, the healing processes will set in, and there will be a trend away from separatism. The questions remaining, it seems, are whether this *will* be done and, if so, whether it will be in time to stop yet another generation of alienated from creating hostile camps that recognize neither compromise nor persuasion.

Index